soft as water

Stories of peace
and hope for you, Thistle.
With all my love, Mom
and Brian

soft as water
is first published 2018
by
Irene Publishing
Sparsnäs 1010
66891 Ed
Sweden
irene.publishing@gmail.com

www.irenepublishing.com

Layout and design: J. Johansen in cooperation with Charles P. Busch

Cover photo and illustrations: Fotograf Johansen & Olsen

ISBN 978-91-88061-25-6

Copyrights and permissions for reuse of quotes from other texts are organised through *The Permissions Group Inc.*

www.permissionsgroup.com

ISBN 978-91-88061-25-6

soft as water

52 Meditations on Peace

by Charles P. Busch

If you don't know the kind of person I am

and I don't know the kind of person you are

a pattern that others made may prevail in the world

and following the wrong god home we may miss our star.

-from "A Ritual to Read to Each Other,"

by William Stafford

Acknowledgements

Astronomer Carl Sagan said, "If you want to make an apple pie from scratch, first you have to create a universe." As I look to thank those who helped in the creation of this book, whole constellations appear: ancient mothers, fathers and saints, contemporary friends and teachers, smart enemies, kind strangers, poets, storytellers, the wise from ten thousand books.

Thank you Al Jubitz and Ray Jubitz of the Jubitz Family Foundation for your friendship, and for making the writing of this book my job description. And thanks to the Core Team of the Foundation's *War Prevention Initiative* for their inspiration and company: Patrick Hiller, Liz Thatcher, Erin Thomas, and Joy Henry.

Thank you to the anonymous donor from the Boston Foundation who funded the start-up of *Fields of Peace* (an ongoing peace education experiment), and the many generous friends who have contributed year after year to continue its work.

Thank you to each of the writers quoted in this collection, with particular thanks to my dear friends and heroes, Romy Ashby, Naomi Shihab Nye, and Kim Stafford.

Thank you to the talented friends who read this book in manuscript and made such valuable suggestions: Romy Ashby, Delta Distad, Ken McCormack, Rev. Frances Menlove, and Julie Otrugman. Thank you to Delta Distad for lending me a home with a view, Alexandra Del Vecchio for her generous surprise gifts, and Tammy Viles for her computer savvy.

Thank you to the thousands of *Peace Village* students, teachers, volunteers, and Board members of 23 years who are family, and give me hope.

Thank you to my brother in the Spirit, Hob, and to my spiritual sister, Olivia, two saints whose lives have shown me, and so many others, the way to peace.

Thank you to my brilliant wife, Cathey, who did the first and ongoing edits to rescue this book, and whose love encouraged me along the way. And thanks to my peacemaker son, Gabriel, who calls me to be responsible to the future.

This book is Dedicated to

Cathey and Gabriel

pure hearts

Introduction

soft as water is a book about peace. It is a call to overcome violence with the soft power at work in us: love, honesty, humility, forgiveness, devotion to justice. The title comes from the *Tao Te Ching*, the ancient book of Chinese wisdom.

> *Nothing in the world*
> *is as soft and yielding as water.*
> *Yet for dissolving the hard and inflexible,*
> *nothing can surpass it.*

To nurture the peace in us, I offer 52 readings which have helped me. They are intended as meditations. Most are excerpts, and come from diverse voices and sources----movies and memoirs, novels and history, folk tales and anecdote. Each is only a page, and can stand alone. You can begin with #1 or simply let the book open where it will. Following each, I offer a brief commentary.

Words about peace, I've found, disturb as much as they comfort. I wish you that good disruption. To begin, here's a Sufi story that is an old friend to me.

> *Nasrudin boarded a train and found a seat. Then came a whistle, a jolt, and the train was on its way.*
>
> *When the conductor came and asked for his ticket, Nasrudin opened his briefcase, but it wasn't there. "Ah," he said, and got out his wallet, but it wasn't there. So he stood and checked his trouser pockets. Nothing.*
>
> *"Sir," the conductor said, "In my experience, most men keep their tickets in the inside left hand pocket of their jackets."*
>
> *"Yes," said Nasrudin, "but if I look there and it isn't there, what hope will I have left?"*

There are many stories in the Sufi tradition about Nasrudin the wise fool. In this one, he's on a journey. I believe it's the same one we're all on: to come to a place of peace.

Each pocket Nasrudin tries is empty. Perhaps they once held tickets which didn't take him anywhere, or took him where he found he didn't want to go.

To continue on his journey, Nasrudin must come up with a ticket. The only pocket left is the warm one, the one closest to the heart. It's the pocket most of us leave for last.

Let's reach in. Reach in.

Charles P. Busch
Lincoln City, Oregon, 2018

Table of Contents

1

From American novelist Kurt Vonnegut's memoir, *Man Without a Country*:

I had just finished giving a reading in Pittsburgh, and a young man came up to me after and said: "Mr. Vonnegut, please tell me it will all be o.k."

"Welcome to Earth, young man," I said. "It's hot in the Summer and cold in the Winter. It's round and wet and crowded. At the outside, Joe, you've got about a hundred years here. There's only one rule that I know of: ...Damn it, Joe, you've got to be kind."

COMMENTARY

The earth is big and half the time it's dark, and we are tiny and can see only so far.

"Will it all be o.k.?"

I like it that Vonnegut doesn't try to reassure Joe. He simply gives him something to do. Not a diversion, as if he were a child, but an assignment, something he or any of us can do: be kind.

Kindness, it seems to me, is what we wait for from one another. It's immediate and warm, and unconcerned with worth. It senses kinship. It says, "Welcome to Earth."

2

In *Early Morning: Remembering My Father, William Stafford*, poet Kim Stafford shares this story about his father as a boy in Kansas in the 1920's:

> *... When he was first in school, he came home to report that two black children on the playground had been taunted by the others.*
>
> *"And what did you do, Billy?" his mother asked.*
>
> *"I went and stood by them."*

COMMENTARY

Little Billy stepped forward, which meant stepping out of the crowd. His footsteps across that playground marked a path which can still be followed.

-He does not remain a passive by-stander, he acts.

-He does not mirror the hurtful behavior, he remains himself.

-Willing to risk suffering, he goes and stands with.

Somehow, Billy knew the most human and ultimately effective way to deal with conflict: the nonviolent way. How natural he makes it seem.

Billy became the poet William Stafford, who wrote,

We live in an occupied country, misunderstood;
justice will take us millions of intricate moves.

from "Thinking for Berky"

3

In a monastery in Russia, an elderly holy man is dying. His name is Fr. Zossima. For decades, pilgrims from all over Russia and Europe have come to receive his healing touch, wisdom, and most of all, his blessing. He is a "staretz," a living saint.

In his final hours, Fr. Zossima calls the monks and novices of the monastery to his bedside. They crowd into his cell to hear his last words. The old saint speaks to them about how to live humbly in the light of God. His voice is weak, hardly more than a whisper, but he speaks for an hour, then two and on into the night. He tells them that he has a childlike conviction that our sufferings will be healed, and at the end, we will experience a great harmony, and all humanity will meet with mercy.

This scene is from Dostoevsky's novel, *The Brothers Karamazov*. I first read it decades ago. But through the years, out of Zossima's flood of words, what stayed with me were three rather plain sentences. Fr. Zossima says:

> *Every day and every hour, every minute, walk round yourself and watch yourself, and see that your image is a seemly one. You pass by a little child, you pass by, spiteful, with ugly words, with wrathful heart; you may not have noticed the child, but he has seen you, and your image, unseemly and ignoble, may remain in his defenseless heart. You don't know it, but you may have sown an evil seed in him and it may grow, and all because you were not careful before the child, because you did not foster in yourself a careful, actively benevolent love.*

COMMENTARY

Father Zossima sets a high standard. Not only are we responsible for our words and actions, but our very way of being. Somehow, the hope or melancholy or anxiety or delight we carry is discernable, even contagious. But how are we to walk around ourselves and see ourselves?

The most helpful advice I've received came from, Yoga Master John Schlorholtz. He said to our ElderSpirit workshop: "Close your eyes. See yourself walking from your car into the grocery store. You are crossing the parking lot. What do you see? Is your chin down, eyes to the ground? Are you leaning forward as if you were pulling a little plow? Are you thinking about getting there, but oblivious to how?

"Nobody teaches us how to walk," John said. "Yet, it's our most basic movement.

"Now imagine you're on vacation. Maybe a warm place in Mexico. You wake up in the morning and go out to get a newspaper. Notice how you walk back to the hotel. You're looking forward to breakfast, but in no hurry. Your shoulders are down, your feet feel the ground. Your arms loose at your side. Breath even. You're looking around, at home, happy in your body.

"That's your vacation walk. That's how to walk all the time."

4

A cover of gray clouds blocks the sun. Bits of ash dot the air. There are no fresh grasses, no leaves on the trees, no birds, no fish, no seasons, and only a scattering of human survivors.

This is the setting of Cormac McCarthy's 2006 novel, *The Road*. It is the story of a father and his seven-year-old son making their way on foot across a cold, silent, barren landscape which has been destroyed by burning, by the kind of devastation which would follow a nuclear holocaust.

The father and son are continually on the brink of starvation, and on alert against the terror of roving bands of road warriors who are cannibals.

> *We wouldn't ever eat anybody, would we? asks the boy.*
> *No. Of course not, says the father.*
> *Even if we were starving?*
> *We're starving now.*
> *You said we weren't.*
> *I said we weren't dying. I didn't say we weren't starving.*
> *But we wouldn't, says the boy.*
> *No. We wouldn't, answers the father.*
> *No matter what.*
> *No. No matter what.*
> *Because we're the good guys.*
> *Yes.*

On the road, all that the father and son have is their love of one another, and the frail hope that leads them south where it is warmer. Pushing a shopping cart with their small store, they continue on.

> **Is the dark going to catch us? asks the boy.**
> **I don't know.**
> **It is, isn't it?**
> **Come on. We'll hurry.**

COMMENTARY

Reading *The Road*, I want to drop the book, jump from my chair and run back to the day before. Before the ending fire, before cities became smoking ruins, before the streams turned black and the mornings silent, before the bands in war paint with their livestock of chained captives.

Before, when there was still time to say NO!

Between August 6, 1945, when the U.S. dropped the first nuclear bomb on Hiroshima, and today, there have been hundreds of crises when our world has been within two or three minutes of a nuclear detonation. They were caused by the inevitable: accidents, miscommunication, human error, mechanical malfunction. They were caused by normalizing insanity.

> *We escaped the Cold War without a nuclear holocaust by some combination of skill, luck, and divine intervention, and I suspect the latter in greatest proportion.*
>
> -Gen. George Butler, head of Strategic Air Command in 1991

> *If nothing fundamental changes, then I would expect the use of nuclear weapons, in some 10 year period, is very possible.*
>
> -Henry Kissinger, 2010, former Secretary of State

> *The acquisition and use of nuclear weapons by a terrorist organization is indeed becoming more likely...In Russia there is particular concern over certain ambiguities regarding suitcase sized "mini-nucs", though even larger nuclear weapons, such as those possessed by Pakistan, could be stolen with a large truck.*
>
> -Nuclear Age Peace Foundation

Today is the day before, when we can still say NO! No to the nine nations who brandish nuclear power. No to proliferation. No to the 168 million dollars a day the U.S. spends to maintain its nuclear arsenal. No to nuclear research and testing. No to the Titan II missile's nine megatons---three times the force of all the bombs dropped in WWII. No to the illusion that the story of *The Road* is not about us.

> ***Is the darkness going to catch us? asks the boy.***
> ***I don't know.***

5

Once upon a time in a mountain valley, there was a village. Like all villages it had a baker and blacksmith, a teacher and a gossip, lots of children, and a tailor. The houses were made of logs and there were gardens and chicken coops. On Sundays the children were given rides on a donkey.

One day a Giant entered the valley. He lived in a hut in the forest, but when the mood struck, he'd go to the village and demand food. He was a huge, shaggy, crude man with a big voice that sounded like the complaint of a donkey.

One afternoon, after a meal of 7 chickens, 12 ears of corn and many bowls of pudding, and after his usual bout of burping and other base sounds, the Giant felt like having a little fun. And just then, the tailor walked by.

"Over here, chicken bones!" shouted the Giant. The tailor was a little man who always wore the same black suit and walked with his chin on his chest. The Giant grabbed him by the collar and marched him to the market place.

People gathered around. They were curious, and glad that the tailor was "it" and not them.

"Who's strongest," shouted the Giant, "me or this spit-out piece of a thing? Let's have a contest. We'll see who can throw the farthest."

The Giant looked around for the right stone---one the size of a grape-fruit. And the tailor looked for something he could throw.

"I'll go first," said the Giant. He took a great breath, leaned back and threw. The villagers gasped. The stone made a great arc, grew small in the air, and came down at the far edge of the village. Boys ran to mark the spot.

Proud and smirking, the Giant said, "Now you!"

The tailor stepped forward, put a hand in his suit pocket, then raised and opened his hand . There, was a gray sparrow. It fluttered, turned its head this way and that, and flew off. It went high and circled over the village, once, twice, then flew off over the forest and disappeared into the gray mist of the mountain.

COMMENTARY

I don't know where I first heard the story of the giant and the tailor. Some stories are too old to have a single source, and threatening giants have always been a problem in the world. They appear in our midst, shout, flex, and demand. They want what we have. And they want us to be small.

We all live this story, and the question it asks is blunt: how are you going to overcome the monster without becoming the monster? This old problem requires, each time, a fresh solution. Like the tailor, our job is to use imagination to come up with a stone with wings.

Like all stories, this one can grow into a larger story. It needn't end with a winner and a loser. All that's needed for the ending to become another beginning are the words, "And then…"

…the villagers became quiet. They stood facing the mountain. No one dared turn and look at the Giant. No one whispered. Even the children were still.

"I'm hungry," the tailor said to the Giant. "Let's go to my house. We'll eat. And I'll make you a hat with a pheasant feather."

The Giant looked at him.

"Also," said the tailor, "I need your help. There's a stream by my house, I need a log over it so I can get across."

6

A few years back, my wife Cathey and I went to South Texas to visit her family. One morning I went to a coffee shop to sit and read the *Times*. Near me was a small group of men about my age, in their 70's. One had on a yellow ball cap, *Caterpillar*, the others were gray-haired and balding. When a latecomer joined them, he was greeted with, "What's new?" He replied, "Same old, war and weather."

The word "war" hit home, and I felt an impulse to go over. I imagined they'd ask where I was from and what I do. I'd say, "The coast of Oregon. I'm a peace educator." We'd talk about the 50's---cars, Elvis, Marilyn. Then the 60's---Vietnam. At least one of them would have been in it. Then somebody'd ask, "What do peace educators do?" I'd keep it light: "We remind each other that we're all in this together."

But I didn't go over. And when they left, I thought about what I really wanted to say. And the words came: "Weather is inevitable, but there's nothing inevitable about war, and not only war, but a single harsh word, shove, or moment of indifference to the suffering of another. Always there is a choice.

COMMENTARY

"Same old, war and weather." How often those words get repeated and the *myths* that accompany them. In his book, *War No More*, David Swanson writes about those myths. Paraphrasing, here are three of them.

Myth One: Humans are violent by nature. Not really. Most people, most of the time, handle conflict without violence. We put up fences, establish laws, try to stay within the speed limit, and practice what works: compromise and cooperation. It's violence that is the aberration.

> *Come, be human. Sit down and let's talk.*
>
> -William Stafford

Myth Two: There has always been war. Not really. In the 200,000 years of human history, there is no evidence of war until the most recent 10,000 years. Wars started when sedentary societies formed, and then only in some of them, some of the time. Today, there are a number of nations who haven't fought wars in centuries, and European nations have been at peace for 65 years. War is simply a social invention which can and needs to be discarded.

> *Armies are a result of obsolete ways---just as gibbets are, and as thumbscrews are, and leper windows.*
>
> -William Stafford

Myth Three: War is necessary to combat evil in the world. Not really. Throughout the world, *war itself* is the great evil: leveler of cities, taker of bread, killer of civilians, maker of refugees. Wars don't make us safer, they plant hate and the desire for revenge, and provide the model for more of the same. Evil cannot be overcome with more evil.

> *How far down the road are you looking? Where you turn off? Where a bridge waits? Into the fog?*
>
> -William Stafford

There is nothing inevitable about war, and not only war, but a single harsh word, shove, or moment of indifference to the suffering of another. Always there is a choice.

7

People are like newspaper, they'll put up with anything you put on them.

-Joseph Stalin

There are no innocent civilians...you are fighting a people, you are not fighting an armed force anymore. So it doesn't bother me so much to be killing the so-called innocent bystanders.

-U.S. General Curtis LeMay, 1944

Mundus vult decipi, ergo decepiatur. The world wants to be deceived, therefore let it be deceived.

-Hitler's favorite Latin proverb

Naturally the common people don't want war: Neither in Russia, nor in England, nor for that matter in Germany. That is understood. But after all, IT IS THE LEADERS of the country who determine the policy and it is always a simple matter to drag the people along, whether it is a democracy, or a fascist dictatorship, or a parliament, or a communist dictatorship. Voice or no voice, the people can always be brought to the bidding of the leaders. That is easy. All you have to do is TELL THEM THEY ARE BEING ATTACKED, and denounce the peacemakers for lack of patriotism and exposing the country to danger. IT WORKS THE SAME IN ANY COUNTRY.

-Herman Goering at the Nuremberg Trials

We had to destroy it to save it.

-U.S. Major Booris, Ben Tre, Vietnam, Feb 7, 1968

Nothing is true, everything is permitted.

-William Burroughs, from *The Cities of the Red Night*

COMMENTARY

I cringe when I read these statements. I hate the cynicism and moral amnesia they sell. Yet I read and list them for others to read. It is way of saying, "Never again."

The voice of cynicism is seductive. It is worldly and knowing. It tells us, "Look out for number one, nobody else will." It frees us to do our worst in fear that others are doing the same.

We've seen where this can take us, the life hating it becomes. Stalin, Goering, Hitler, were mass murderers.

General Curtis LeMay, who commanded the U.S. firebombing of 67 Japanese cities at the close of WWII, was wrong: women and children and the old are innocent.

> *Summon the principle that no statement*
> *should be made that could not be made*
> *in the presence of the burning children.*
>
> -Irving Greenberg commenting on the Holocaust

Cynicism, my own and that of others, leaves me in need of a word of simple goodness, a reminder that we are and can be good again.

> *Innocence rises from human beings*
> *like steam from hot food...*
>
> -from "Morning Psalms," by Yehuda Amichai

8

Willie Morris was editor of *Harpers Magazine*, but is best known for his autobiographical novel, *My Dog Skip*. The scene below is from the movie of the same title.

The year is 1942, the place Yazoo, Mississippi. Willie is eight years old. His hero and next door neighbor is Dink Jenkins, who was varsity captain of all the teams at Yazoo High School. On the day of graduation, Dink and his buddies joined the Army and were sent overseas to fight the Germans.

A year later, Dink returned home, but at night. So unlike the send-off parade when he and his pals waved from a convertible to all the folks waving flags along Main Street. Everybody in town knows Dink is home and holed up in his parents' house drinking. Word is, he was dishonorably discharged for cowardice.

Young Willie refuses to believe what folks are saying. One afternoon he spots Dink sitting on the front steps of his house, and Willie goes over and sits next to him. Willie's wearing the red baseball cap with the letter "Y" on it that Dink gave him on the day of the parade.

> *"You think I don't know what folks are sayin'?" Dink says. 'That ole Dink's a coward.' Huh? Well I know. And you know what? They're right. I got scared and ran. You think it's cause I was afraid of dyin'? Cause I wished I was dead plenty of times."*
>
> *Willie looks up at Dink. "Then what was it?"*
>
> *"It ain't the dyin' that's scary boy. It's the killin'."*

COMMENTARY

Dink is the first of his kind in Yazoo, the first to run from war. What led him to run in the midst of combat wasn't fear of death. He ran from revulsion, not only of blood and torn bodies, but of himself and what he saw of humankind.

"It's the killin'."

The home town folks don't understand what's happened to their high school hero, but neither does he. So Dink drinks. There's a lot to dull and quell, and mourn. He's lost his old buddies, old world, old self. And there are so many dead left behind.

What's true can look to us at first like its opposite. Courage can look like cowardice. Honesty like betrayal. A hero like a traitor. The beginning of something like the end of everything.

Dink is the first of his kind in Yazoo.

For now, Dink sits on the steps. He's no longer at home upstairs in his parents' house, but not yet ready to step down onto the road and where it leads. He's on the steps, the in between place.

9

Hillel was a Jewish sage (110 BCE −10 CE) who founded a world-renown school in Jerusalem, the House of Hillel. When he died at the age of 120, he was the spiritual leader of Israel.

Today, he is a legend, and many stories are told about him, his holiness, and wisdom. I like to tell this one:

One day in the market place, a gentile man came up to Hillel and challenged him. "Tell me the Torah while standing on one foot."

How was Hillel to answer? How could anyone give the entire message of the five books of Moses, the Mishna, the Gamara, the law and oral tradition which comprise the Torah, in the length of time an old man can stand on one foot?

Hillel was a humble man, and took the stranger's challenge as a sincere inquiry. He lifted his right foot and said:

> *What is hateful to you, do not do to your fellow man.*
> *That is the whole of the Torah. The rest is commentary.*
> *Go study.*

COMMENTARY

In one form or another, most of us know the Golden Rule. As a child I was taught, "Do not treat others as you would not like them to treat you." The point was respectful behavior beyond family and friends, extending even to enemies. Like the gentile man, it was up to me to "go and learn" how to live it.

What I've learned in 70 years of life is that the yearning that runs deep in me runs deep in us all: the yearning for peace in the world, peace in our relationships, and peace within ourselves. What is "hateful" to me is anything that hinders that peace.

Like the gentile man, I want a sage, and have a request: "While standing on one foot, tell me how to be peace in the world."

Is there a sage in our day who has answered? I believe there is.

Daniel Berrigan (1921 – 2016), was a Jesuit priest, poet, scholar, and anti-war activist. In June, 1980, he stood in a Pennsylvania courtroom about to be sentenced to prison. The crime: he and seven others had entered a secret General Electric nuclear factory, and hammered two unarmed warheads and poured blood, their own, over them. This became known as the Plowshares Act. Standing on two feet, Berrigan said:

> *It's terrible for me to live in a time where I have nothing to say to human beings except, "Stop killing." There are other beautiful things I would love to be saying to people. But I cannot. Because everything is endangered. Everything is up for grabs. Our plight is very primitive from a Christian point of view. We are back where we started. Thou shalt not kill: we are not allowed to kill. Everything today comes down to that – everything.*

10

In 1942, in Hamburg, Germany, a group of 500 middle-aged men were drafted into what was called "Reserve Police Battalion 101."

Only a few of these were policemen. Some were business men, others dock workers, truck drivers, machine operators, waiters, druggists, teachers.

This group of ordinary men were put in uniform, given a quick orientation, and then sent to take part in the Nazis' "Final Solution in Poland," the eradication of all Jews.

When the Battalion arrived, they were told that their duty was to round up Jews from the ghettos and force them onto trains. The destination was Treblinka and its gas chambers. When trains were unavailable, however, the Jews were taken into the countryside, forced to dig trenches, and shot in the head.

This became the work of Reserve Police Battalion 101: shooting, at point-blank range, old men, women, and children. There were days when they killed as many as 14,000 Jews. The details of this human slaughter are ghastly and indelible.

Yet, only a handful of the 500 men conscripted into Battalion 101 said, "No."

After the war, the men from that battalion returned to their former "ordinary" lives. In the 1960's, nearly 20 years after the War, the State Prosecutor of Hamburg interviewed 210 men who had served in the battalion.

The men were blunt in their comments. Most said they felt pressure to conform and feared that if they didn't carry out the killing, they would suffer punishment and certainly damage to their reputations and civilian careers. They spoke of only doing their duty and felt that any moral responsibility belonged to those above them who gave the orders.

Only a few were ever prosecuted for war crimes.

COMMENTARY

This is the twentieth century,
you are there, preparing to skin
a human being alive. Your part
will be to remain calm.

-from "A First on TV" by David Ignatow

Reading about Police Battalion 101, I want their atrocities to be the behavior of a few psychopaths or the terrible flaw of the people of another country. I want to believe in my own goodness, and that of others.

When I was a young man, I had a friend and business partner who was Jewish. One day, talking together about the Holocaust, he asked, "If you saw them come for me, would you step out your door and go with me? "Yes," I said, and meant it. Today, I have a wife and child. Remembering his question, I pause.

Philosopher, Hannah Arendt, describes a Nazi functionary as one who "does not regard himself as a murderer because he has not done it out of inclination but in his professional capacity. Out of sheer passion he would never do harm to a fly." This was confirmed by the men of Reserve Police Battalion 101 who, years after the war, excused themselves of responsibility by claiming they were simply following orders.

The story of Police Battalion 101 serves notice. War crimes are committed by ordinary and ordinarily decent people. Arendt calls this "the banality of evil." These crimes take place in every war on every side. They tell of the crime which is war.

The first casualty of war is our humanity.

11

Laurens van der Post---novelist, philosopher, explorer, farmer, soldier, conservationist---was born in 1906 to English parents in the outback of South Africa on the edge of the great Kalahari Desert. As a boy, he came to know and befriend the aboriginal Bushman whom he called "First Man." Van der Post learned their language, walked their trackless landscape, and by campfire, was entrusted with their sacred stories. He writes,

First man, as I knew him and his history, was a remarkable, gentle being, fierce only in defense of himself and the life of those in his keeping. He had no legends or stories of great wars among his own kind and regarded the killing of another human being except in self-defense as the ultimate depravity of his spirit.

I was told a most moving story of how a skirmish between two clans, in which just one man was killed on a long-forgotten day, caused them to renounce armed conflict forever.

Van der Post goes on to claim that the remarkable gentleness of the Bushman is not unique to them, but a divine impulse for unity at work in every human being.

The Bushman was living proof to me of how the pattern of the individual in service of a self that is the manifestation of the divine in humankind was built into life at the beginning and will not leave our kind and the earth alone until it is fulfilled.

It is no mere intellectual or ideological concept, but a primary condition written into the contract of life with the creator.

COMMENTARY

With the Bushmen in the Kalahari, Van der Post glimpsed something of humankind's first morning. To walk the sands of that desert, to kneel in the mud of a sip-well and suck water through a reed, to follow a honey bird to its tree, to be still in the presence of a praying mantis, was to step into a timeless story.

He describes these primitive, nomadic people as "gentle." So gentle, that it struck him as the print of the divine in human nature.

> *The Bushman was living proof of the individual in service of a self...*
> *a self that is the manifestation of the divine in humankind.*

Van der Post's claim of humankind's inherent aversion to violence confronts history and the dark reality of the 20th century: two World Wars, the Holocaust and Hiroshima.

But Van der Post was not naïve. He fought as a British Officer in WWII and survived two years as a Japanese prisoner of war in Soekaboemi, a Javanese jungle camp. There he experienced beatings, torture, starvation, and witnessed beheadings of his own troops. Yet, what he knew of "First Man" remained true for him. Why? Because, I believe, it matched the reverence and deep sense of connectedness which was undeniable in his own heart.

> *...a primary condition written into the contract of life with the creator.*

Reverence for this contract led the Bushmen to renounce armed conflict forever, and trust that:

> *...the divine in humankind will not leave our kind and the earth alone*
> *until it is fulfilled.*

12

In the Hebrew Bible in Genesis, we are told that the first man, Adam, knew his wife Eve, and she bore a son Cain, and then a second son Abel.

Now Abel was a keeper of sheep, and Cain a tiller of the ground. In the course of time Cain brought to the Lord an offering of the fruit of the ground, and Abel for his part brought of the firstlings of his flock, their fat portions. And the Lord had regard for Abel and his offering, but for Cain and his offering he had no regard.

So Cain was very angry, and his countenance fell. The Lord said to Cain, "Why are you angry, and why has your countenance fallen? If you do well, will you not be accepted? And if you do not do well, sin is lurking at the door; its desire is for you, but you must master it."

Cain said to his brother Abel, "Let us go out to the field." And when they were in the field, Cain rose up against his brother Abel, and killed him. Then the Lord said to Cain, "Where is your brother Abel?" He said, "I do not know; am I my brother's keeper? And the Lord said, "What have you done? Listen; your brother's blood is crying out to me from the ground! And now you are cursed from the ground, which has opened its mouth to receive your brother's blood from your hand. When you till the ground, it will no longer yield to you its strength; you will be a fugitive and a wanderer on the earth."

COMMENTARY

Each time I read the story of Cain and Abel, I look for the secret of *why* we, humankind, are so given to violence. Instead, I am shown something else: that it need not be so.

In the story, God judges Cain twice. First, for something lacking in his harvest offering, and second, for killing his brother. But Cain had no stone tablet of Commandments to go by, no book of scripture in which his duty to God and brother are spelled out. On what grounds does God find him guilty?

My guess is *conscience*---the knowing in Cain's heart, as in every heart, of what is right and wrong, just and unjust. But conscience is soft spoken.

What was lacking when Cain placed his bouquet of wheat on the altar? Gratitude. His barn was full, he felt proud and self-sufficient. He didn't want to hear about the sun and the rain and the mystery in the seed that made the harvest possible.

Why did Cain answer God's question about Abel's whereabouts with the evasion, "Am I my brother's keeper?" Because Cain *knew* what he had done was wrong, and didn't want to admit it.

Cain was guilty because in his heart he knew right attitude from wrong, and right action from wrong.

When I lean in and listen to my conscience, I hear more than a "yes" or "no." I hear, "Through this one act, something in the world will change or not change. That something may determine what's possible or not possible for all."

***

When the maze and melons wither in the field before summer is out, the high desert people of the San Ildefonso Pueblo dance. Drawn by the soft thunder of drums, the old and the young come to the open ground at the center of the pueblo where the kiva is. From morning to evening and on through the night, they dance. Tireless, stepping to the drum, knowing they are beautiful, they say, "If our hearts are right, if our hearts are right, the rain will come."

13

When Camilo Mejia was 22, he joined the U. S. Army. His family had immigrated to the U.S. from Nicaragua when he was a teen, and he was eager to become a citizen and further his education.

During his three-year enlistment, 1997 to 2000, he earned the rank of Staff Sergeant and continued his service with the Florida National Guard while attending community college. Then, in 2003, his Guard Unit was called to duty in Iraq. There, Mejia received commendations for his leadership of an infantry squad in combat.

While home on two week furlough, what Mejia experienced in Iraq caught up with him: the firefights, ambushes, an innocent man decapitated by machine-gun fire, the torture and mock executions he'd witnessed.

He knew he could no longer participate.

Refusing redeployment in March, 2004, he turned himself in to his Commanding Officer and requested status as a Conscientious Objector. Mejia was the first in the Iraq War to do so, and among the troops he lived with he became an object of hate and harassment.

Mejia also dealt with questions---those of his own stirred conscience, and the charged words of others. When asked the "Hitler question," Mejia answered with a question:

> *People ask, what would have happened if Hitler were not stopped? Well, what would have happened if there had been enough CO's in the Nazi Army? There would have been no War. And no Holocaust.*
>
> *Will there ever be enough CO's to stop an Army? If we don't believe, how are we going to survive as a human race?*

Mejia's request for CO status was denied, and he was court-martialed. At Fort Stewart, Georgia, May 21, 2004, Camilo Mejia was convicted of desertion, sentenced to one year in the Ft. Sill, Kansas military prison, and issued a Bad Conduct Discharge. He said,

> *I was a coward, not for leaving the War, but for having been part of it in the firstplace.*

COMMENTARY

At the close of World War II, the U.S. and the Allies tried Nazi leaders for their war crimes. These tribunals were held in 1945-46 in Nuremberg, Germany. Routinely, the defendants claimed they were *not guilty* because they were following orders which it was their sworn duty to do. This became known, and infamous, as The Nuremberg Defense.

The court judged these defendants *guilty* on the grounds that sworn duty is superseded by the authority of one's own conscience. Ultimately, each person is responsible to say "No" when faced with a crime against humanity.

Camilo Mejia said "No" to killing, torture, and the Iraq War. He did so on the grounds of conscience. The U.S. military court found him *guilty* of not obeying orders. The contradiction in this judgment with military precedent was articulated by former U.S. Attorney General, Ramsey Clark, who was part of Mejia's defense team:

> *What an incredible irony that we're prosecuting soldiers in Iraq for violations of international law* (such as torture at Abu Ghraib Prison) *and we're prosecuting a soldier here because he refused to do the same things.*

The dilemma is real. A military cannot function if orders can be refused. Yet, a person cannot be true to his or her humanity if conscience---the authority of one's inner voice--- is abdicated.

Conscience is real. Like natural law which orders light into a rainbow spectrum beginning with the color red, conscience provides an inherent moral order beginning with the knowledge that each person's life is unique, needed, and sacred.

Although Camilo Mejia was not aware of it, the day he was sentenced to prison in 2004, his answer to the Hitler question was already becoming a reality. In Germany that same year, 150,000 young people were called up to mandatory national service. Of these, 70,000 served as soldiers, but the majority, 80,000, chose to be Conscientious Objectors serving in nonmilitary institutions.

14

Stanley Kunitz, American poet and a Jew, wrote a poem in honor of Dietrich Bonhoeffer, the German Christian martyr. Bonhoeffer was imprisoned during WWII at Tegel and Buchenwald, and hung at Flossenburg concentration camp on April 9, 1945. His crimes: smuggling Jews into Switzerland, spying, creating an underground seminary, preaching sedition, and involvement in a plot to assassinate Hitler.

Next to Last Things

Slime, in the grains of the State,
like smut in the corn,
from the top infected.
Hatred made law,
wolves bred out of maggots
rolling in blood,
and the seal of the church ravished
to receive the crooked sign.
All the steeples were burning.
In the chapel of his ear
he had heard the midnight bells
jangling: if you permit
this evil, what is the good
of the good of your life.
And he forsook the last things,
the dear inviolable mysteries---
Plato's lamp, passed from the hand
of saint to saint---

14 continue

that he might risk his soul in the streets,
where the things given
are only next to last;
In God's name cheating, pretending,
playing the double agent,
choosing to trade
the prayer for the deed,
and the deed most vile.
I am a liar and a traitor.

From Around Pastor Bonhoeffer, by Stanley Kunitz

COMMENTARY

What is a citizen's duty in a time of war? Dietrich Bonhoeffer answered that question with his life: the duty of conscience, whatever the cost.

Bonhoeffer was born into German aristocracy. His family was accomplished, close knit, and saw service to others as their responsibility. As a young theologian, Dietrich prepared for a life of writing, teaching and ministry.

But with Hitler's appointment as chancellor in 1933, and the rapid cutting off of civil liberties and enactment of laws against Jews, Bonhoeffer, who loved his country, felt compelled to speak out. In a radio address shortly after Hitler took power, he called on German Christians to:

> *Question the state. Aid victims of the state, even if they are*
> *not Christians. Work against the state if necessary.*

When the Lutheran and Catholic Churches were co-opted by Hitler, Bonhoeffer helped found the "Confessing Church," an alternative body which refused to be part of the Reich Church. Then, he created an underground seminary to train the next generation of pastors.

> *There is no way to peace along the way of safety.*
> *For peace must be dared, it is itself the great venture and can never be safe.*

The list of crimes made legal in Nazi Germany is the old list of power possessed: arrests without charges, secret prisons, torture, assassinations, preemptive wars; and all this accompanied by a rhetoric of "freedom" and idolatry of the flag.

What did a patriot look like in Germany in the 1930's and 40's? The same as a patriot today. Not the one in step. Not the one who says, "My country right or wrong." But the one who hears, *"If you permit this evil, what is the good of the good of your life?"*, and then acts.

15

The Pathans are a mountain people in northern India who for centuries controlled the Kyber Pass and are infamous fighters. In their tradition, personal honor is an obsession and even slights can require blood revenge.

During colonial rule in India, the Pathans conducted guerrilla warfare against the British for 80 years. Then, a leader emerged named Abdul Ghaffar Khan, a Muslim and son of a powerful tribal chief. Khan was drawn to the teachings of Gandhi, a Hindu, and in 1929, traveled to southern India to meet him.

Influenced by the power of Gandhi's message of nonviolence, the Khan, called "Badshah Khan" (King of Khans), implored his people to see beyond their borders, beyond their religious affiliations, and understand themselves as part of the unity of the people of India.

"Why not," the Khan said, "fight the British, but as an army of nonviolent soldiers, drilled and disciplined. An army pledged to fight, not with guns, but with their lives."

Calling themselves the "Servants of God (Khudai Khidmatgaurs)," the Pathans formed history's first professional nonviolent army. Any Pathan man could join, provided he took the army's oath, which included these words:

I promise to refrain from violence and from taking revenge.
I promise to forgive those who oppress me or treat me with cruelty.

Throughout the 1930's and early forties, one hundred thousand nonviolent Pathan soldiers endured mass shootings, torture, the destruction of their fields, orchards, cattle and homes, jail, flogging, and other humiliations. The Badshah Kahn himself was imprisoned by the British for five years. Yet, the "Servants of God" stood unmoved by the violence inflicted on them, laid down their lives in large numbers, and helped gain the freedom of India, as well, as their own personal transformation.

15 continue

There is nothing surprising in a Muslim or a Pathan like me subscribing to the creed of nonviolence. It is not a new creed. It was followed fourteen-hundred years ago by the Prophet all the time he was in Mecca, and it has since been followed by all those who wanted to throw off an oppressor's yoke.

But we had so far forgotten it that when Gandiji placed it before us, we thought he was sponsoring a novel creed.

—Badshah Khan

COMMENTARY

I wonder why the story of the Badshah Khan and history's first professional nonviolent army---a dramatic, significant, inspiring story---is so little known.

Perhaps because Gandhi's story is so large. Perhaps because it's nearly impossible to imagine Pathan men standing still as British soldiers insulted, beat, and shot them and the brother next to them. Perhaps because, regardless of historical fact, we are fixed in our view of nonviolence as the way of those who live on their knees.

Perhaps because it's a story about Muslims.

Only by luck did I learn about the Badshah Khan. I was reading a book on meditation by Hindu teacher Eknath Easwaran and saw, in a list of his writings, an intriguing title: *A Man to Match His Mountains*. In it, Easwaran tells the story of Abdul Ghaffar Khan's transformation from traditional warrior to nonviolent leader, and his far-seeing commitment to the education of his people, equality of women, and Hindu-Muslim unity. Easwaran also observes that the Khan *erased three myths*:

* That nonviolence can be followed only by those who are gentle

* That nonviolence cannot work against ruthless repression

* That nonviolence has no place in Islam

16

Anticipating his 85th birthday, my father decided to host his own celebration at a fine restaurant. He invited 40 family and friends, and asked that, following dinner, my sister and I each say a few words.

What to say about this man I loved and admired? I could tell about Paul Busch's life as a journalist and professor; and about how the people of Howells, Nebraska, where he grew up, honored him at their Centennial Celebration as "Favorite Son." I could tell how, after graduate school at Columbia, he turned down a job offer at the *New York Times* because he knew my mother didn't want to live there. And never told her! I could hold up his sheer goodness, and the fact that he was beloved by so many.

Then, it came to me. My father had a trait which was utterly unique and remarkable and which, in my 55 years of knowing him, I hadn't seen until now.

At the dinner, following my sister's tribute, I said,

> *How lucky I am to have Paul Busch as my father, and to have all these years as an adult to know and enjoy him. But it was this week, thinking about what I would say tonight, that I saw something in him I'd never noticed, something astonishing. Why hadn't I seen it before? Perhaps because, like storytelling, it was such an obvious a part of who he is. What I saw was this: In all the years I've known him, I never heard my father say a word in praise of himself. Not once. Nothing to make himself shine in the eyes of others. On the other hand, in all those years, I never heard him say a negative word about himself. Not even, "that was stupid of me."*

> *You know him, you know I'm not exaggerating.*

> *What I don't know, is what to call this trait? Radical Sanity? Maybe. But still, that's not quite it. Perhaps you will know what to call it.*

COMMENTARY

"My goal is to become zero."

When I read those words of Mahatma Gandhi, I had the term I needed.

A zero is free of plus or minus signs. My father didn't see himself as more than others, and not less. Just zero. The nothing out of which creation comes.

I like the shape of a zero, it's an oval. It stands upright and completes itself.

Like a circle, it lets the light through. Unlike a circle, it doesn't ask to be perfect.

Being zero, I believe, came naturally to my father. A matter of grace. But for most of us, including Gandhi, it's a practice.

No word or pose in self-promotion,

no word or gesture of self-deprecation

Zero.

17

On the first page of his masterpiece, *Thus Spoke Zarathustra*, philosopher Friedrich Nietzsche states that human beings are capable of three transformations of the spirit through metamorphosis. To explain this, he uses symbols.

We begin, he says, as a CAMEL. In our youth, we are loaded up with rules, mores, laws, the expectations of our culture. We bow to this. Then, rising from our knees, do what Camels and adolescents do, we head out into the desert to find our own way.

There, with luck, we find our voice, Roar. We claim our authority, and are transformed from Camel to LION. The task of the Lion is to kill the dragon whose name is "Thou Shalt Not." On each of the dragon's scales is written a law. Having killed the dragon, the Lion eats, takes in the laws which are life-giving and leaves the rest in the sand.

Many of us never get beyond the Camel stage. We labor under the expectations of others and our given culture. Of those who become Lions, most remain so. The authority of one's own voice, the muscle, the size of one's own head, and the taste of blood entrances.

Only a few, says Nietzsche, manage the third and final metamorphosis: The transformation from Lion to CHILD. The Child is the one who, through vulnerability, brings out in others the love which has been waiting in them.

COMMENTARY

Reading Nietzsche's declaration of the Child as the ultimate expression of the human spirit, I remember the Hebrew story of the Pharaoh's daughter finding an infant in a reed basket on the Nile River. She knows it is a forbidden male child of Hebrew slaves, but he is crying and tiny and helpless. She lifts him up, and has him brought to the palace. The love which the child *evokes* in her, erases in an instant the borders of law, class, race, blood and religion. She names him Moses (meaning, "to draw out"), and raises him as her own son.

The Child is the one in our midst who says, "Will you claim me? Care for me? Love me? Otherwise I cannot live." It is the Child, in its helplessness, who calls forth the love which has been waiting in us to be expressed and realized.

To evolve from Lion to Child is to give up the obvious power of authority and might in favor of the paradoxical power of vulnerability. To do this is daunting. It means risking loss, rejection, perhaps injury. It means trusting what is deepest in ourselves is also there and waiting in others. It trusts that "heart calls to heart" and is heard.

It is the Child who makes of us a family.

18

Whereas the world is a house on fire;
Whereas the nations are filled with shouting;
Whereas hope seems small, sometimes
     a single bird on a wire
     left by migration behind.
Whereas kindness is seldom in the news
     and peace an abstraction
     while war is real;
Whereas my words are all I have;
Whereas my life is short;
Whereas I am afraid;
Whereas I am free---despite all
     fire and anger and fear;
Be it therefore resolved a song
     shall be my calling---a song
     not yet made shall be vocation
     and peaceful words the work
     of my remaining days.

-Kim Stafford

COMMENTARY

In the language of proclamation, in the tradition of the poet, Kim Stafford gives us not news, but honesty. He says aloud what is so hard to admit: violence---its momentum, appetite, its incorporation---is consuming us. *The world is a house on fire...*

To shout "fire" in a crowded theater when there is no fire is a crime. Equally criminal is to fail to shout in a time of crisis. Kim Stafford stands on his seat and shouts, "Fire!" Then, implausibly, beautifully, he takes up his guitar and sings,

> *How would it be to be the last of your kind,*
> *lonesome for the many you once knew?*
>
> *How would it be to see a million stars*
> *and know your nights are few?*

Kim's voice is gentle, and familiar as a brother's voice. And it carries. His song is called "The Lucky Ones." He sings our survival.

> *What if we were few, scattered like the dew*
> *that gathers by dark on the ground?*
>
> *What if every soul made a song of what it knew*
> *and passed it round and round?*

19

In the 300 year history of the U.S. Marine Corps, Smedley Butler is one of only two Marines who received two Medals of Honor.

His combat career began in 1898, in the Spanish-American War, and thirty-three years later, in 1931, he retired as a Major General. His troops called him, "Ole Gimlet Eye," and the Navy commissioned a destroyer in his name: *The USS Butler*.

In retirement, however, Gen. Butler engaged in a different kind of combat: he outed the collusion between big business and government as the prime mover behind U.S. wars.

In the 1930's, he toured the U.S., visiting 700 cities and giving 1,200 speeches. He also published a book, *War Is a Racket*, naming names and documenting how the American "military machine" was used primarily for the benefit of wealthy American industrialists. Butler said:

War is a racket! It always has been. It is possibly the oldest, easily the most profitable, surely the most vicious. It is the only one international in scope. It is the only one in which the profits are reckoned in dollars and the losses in lives.

I spent 33 years in the Marines….most of my time being a high-class muscle man for Big Business, for Wall Street and the Bankers. In short, I was a racketeer, a gangster for capitalism.

I helped make Mexico and especially Tampico safe for American oil interests in 1914. I helped make Haiti and Cuba a decent place for the National City Bank boys to collect revenues in. I helped in the raping of half a dozen Central American republics for the benefit of Wall Street. I helped purify Nicaragua for the International Banking House of Brown Brothers in 1902-1912. I brought light to the Dominican Republic for the American sugar interests in 1916. I helped make Honduras right for the American fruit companies in 1903. In China in 1927, I helped see to it that Standard Oil went on its way unmolested.

19 continue

The bankers collected their profits. But the soldier pays the biggest part of the bill. If you don't believe this, visit the American cemeteries on the battle fields abroad. Or visit any of the veterans' hospitals in the U.S.

COMMENTARY

Gen. Butler pointed to an arrangement of power behind the structures of government, a way of doing things which had become ingrained and too profitable to admit. It was a secret at odds with a nation's righteous sense of self.

Another retired general, in the generation following Butler, offered a similar warning, though in more measured words. In his "Cross of Iron" speech in 1953, President Dwight Eisenhower coined the term "military-industrial complex," and spoke of its social and ethical impact:

> *Every gun that is made, every warship launched, every rocket fired signifies, in the final sense, a theft from those who hunger and are not fed, those who are cold and are not clothed.*

Eisenhower urged Americans to break away from their reliance on military might and "use our power in the interests of world peace and human betterment." His words were not heeded.

In 2018, $597.1 billon will go to military spending. This is one half of our nation's entire annual budget. The United States, with more than 760 military bases beyond its borders, is an Empire that requires ongoing war: Korea, Vietnam, Panama, Granada, Bosnia, The Gulf War, Afghanistan, Iraq, ISIS...

Gen. Butler said, "War is a Racket," and named names. So must we: Bechtel, Lockheed-Martin, General Atomics, General Electric, Carlyle Group, Boeing, Northrop Grumman, Halliburton, Caterpillar... Plus, banks too big to fail, and international oil giants.

I suggest that Smedley Butler be awarded a posthumous *third* Medal of Honor.

20

Maria Jose Hobday (1925-2009) was a Seneca-Iroquois elder and Sister of the Franciscan Order. She called herself a "student of life" and a "missionary-at-large." She shared this anecdote about herself:

One summer Saturday morning when I was twelve, I was waiting for my friend Juanita to come over. We had planned a morning together, and she was quite late. I was fretting and complaining, and generally making a nuisance of myself. Finally, my father said to me, "Get a book, a blanket, and an apple, and get into the car."

I obeyed. My father drove me about eight miles from home to a canyon area, and said, "Now get out. We cannot stand you any longer at home! You aren't fit to live with. Just stay out here by yourself today until you understand better how to act. I'll be back this evening."

I got out, angry, frustrated, and defiant. I thought immediately of walking home; eight miles was no distance at all for me. Then the thought of meeting my father when I got there took hold. I cried and threw the book, apple and blanket over the canyon ledge.

But it was hard to keep up a good, rebellious cry with no audience. I sat on the rim, kicking the dirt and trying to get control of myself. After a couple of hours, I began to get hungry. I located the apple and climbed down to retrieve it---as well as the book and the blanket. I climbed back up, and noticed the pinion tree. It was lovely and full. I spread the blanket in the shade, put the book under my head, and began to eat the apple.

20 continue

I was aware of a change of attitude. As I looked through the branches into the sky, a great sense of peace and beauty came to me. The clouds sat in still puffs, the blue was endless, and I began to take in their spaciousness. I thought about the way I had acted and why Daddy had treated me so harshly. I found myself getting in touch with my feelings, with the world around me. Nature was my mother, holding me for comfort and healing. I became aware of being part of it all, and found myself thinking of God. I wanted harmony. I wanted to hold the feeling of mystery. I wanted to be a better person.

It was a prayerful time, a time of deep silence. I felt in communion with much that I could not know, but to which I was drawn. I had a great sense of discovering myself as great, of seeing the world as great, of touching the holy. This sense lasted a long time, perhaps a couple of hours.

COMMENTARY

When I'm hurting and feel defeated, something in me knows to seek a quiet place apart. I want to let a larger beauty in.

But it's not so simple. Whether I'm in a canyon setting or a little room with a candle, the moment I sit down my mind begins to mock. "Really? You're just going to sit here?" And back of this, is the fear of what I might *hear* in that silence, what might be asked of me.

So, like Maria, I must be driven there. If not by a father, a friend who confronts me. Or the shock of hard news from a doctor. Or failure. Or the death of someone I love. Or, the good news of the birth of a child, or the words, "I love you too."

Hobday's story reminds me that seeking a quiet place apart is a *practice*, required practice. Moses went to the mountain top. The Buddha sat under the Bodhi tree. Jesus sought a place apart. Muhammad entered a cave.

There, what is thrown over the canyon edge is not a book or an apple, but the *self*. And what is retrieved is a larger self. Maria describes it:

> *I had a great sense of discovering myself as great,*
> *of seeing the world as great, of touching the holy.*

21

Mohandas Gandhi, the nonviolent revolutionary whose movement ended British rule in India without firing a shot, was assassinated on January 30, 1948. He was on his way to evening prayers. His killer was Nathuram Godse.

During the murder trial, Godse justified his action by citing the *Bhagavad Gita*, a sacred Hindu scripture.

The *Gita* is a 700-verse dialogue between Arjuna, a young warrior, and Krishna, an incarnation of God who has been sent to him as counselor. The conversation takes place on the eve of a battle between two factions of the same tribe: The Pandavas (Arjuna's side) and the Kauravas. Arjuna is scared and troubled; he does not wish to kill his cousins and elders.

Speaking to the court, Godse explained that his act was modeled on the nobility of Arjuna:

> *My respect for the Mahatma was deep and deathless. It therefore gave me no pleasure to kill him. Indeed my feelings were like those of Arjuna when he killed Dronacharya, his Guru at whose feet he had learnt the art of war. But the Guru stood with the Kauravas and for that reason he felt no compunction in finishing his revered Guru. Before doing so, however, he first threw an arrow at the feet of Dronacharya as a mark of respect for the Guru; the second arrow he aimed at the chest of the Guru and finished him. My feelings towards Gandhi were similar. I hold him first in the highest respect and therefore on January 30, I bowed to him first, then at point blank range fired three successive shots and killed him. My provocation was his constant and consistent pandering to the Muslims. I had no private grudge, no self-interest, no sordid motive in killing him. It was his provocation, over a period of twenty years, which finally exhausted my patience; and my inner voice urged me to kill him, which I did. I am not asking for any mercy.*

COMMENTARY

Both Gandhi and Godse were Hindu and looked to the *Bhagavad Gita* as their scripture and daily guide. And both aspired to its teaching of anasakti, selfless action.

What then divided them?

It was, I believe, the fault line which runs through each religion between those who take the words of scripture *literally* and those who understand them *metaphorically, allegorically, symbolically.*

Gandhi understood the *battlefield* in the Gita to be a metaphor for the human heart where the war between right and wrong is waged. He read the *dialogue between* Arjuna and Krishna as the interior conversation in which the self questions the Self about self-mastery.

Godse, however, took the scene of Arjuna's killing of his cousin Dronacharya as a blueprint of how to deal with conflict, a literal instruction to kill those seen to side with evil, not excluding those closest to us. Rather than clear his own heart, he chose to clear the world.

The central message of the *Gita*, writes Hindu scholar Eknath Easwaran, is to see the Lord in every creature and act accordingly.

Seeing the same Lord everywhere, they do not harm themselves or others.

–Gita 13:27-28

Godse bowed to Gandhi before pulling the trigger of his revolver, but he didn't bow low enough. He saw the saint in Gandhi, but failed to see the Lord.

22

A Cherokee elder is sharing wisdom with his grandson. "A fight is going on inside me," he says to the boy. "It is a terrific fight, and it is between two wolves.

"*One is evil.* He is anger, envy, sorrow, regret, greed, arrogance, self-pity, guilt, resentment, inferiority, lies, false pride, superiority, and ego.

"*The other is good.* He is joy, peace, love, hope, serenity, humility, kindness, benevolence, empathy, generosity, truth, compassion, and faith.

"The same fight is going on inside you, and inside every person, too."

The grandson thinks about his grandfather's words, then asks, "Which wolf will win?"

He replies, "The one you feed."

COMMENTARY

There are times when I find it difficult, maybe impossible, to believe in the essential goodness of humankind. I've seen too much intentional cruelty, and indifference to the suffering others. And, the recurring madness of war. I also know too well the shadows at home in my own heart.

The Cherokee elder offers a wisdom which is practical and empowering: we become good by practicing goodness. The heart is neither divided nor whole, but an open space. What prevails there is what we entertain:

> The thoughts we hold. Stories we tell. Company we keep. Heroes we look to.
> The forgiveness we extend. Simplicity we practice. Books we read.
> The scripture we turn to. Songs we sing. Prayers we pray.
> The walks we take. The silence we keep.
> The silence we refuse to keep.

23

In WWI, the ratio of deaths
combatants to civilian was
9 to 1.
In WWII, the ratio became
1 to 1.
In today's wars, the ratio is
1 to 9.
Today, far more children die
in war than combatants.

War has become the killing
of children.

-Graca Machel, "Impact of Armed Conflict on Children," 2016

-"American Journal of Public Health," June, 2014

-Richard Goldstone, "Stanford Report," Jan 2011

COMMENTARY

Each morning when I walk my dog, I stop at a spot overlooking the ocean and say out loud a Promise. It begins,

I will not be a part of the killing
of any child,

Overheard, these words may sound strange, but they are my response to learning that today's wars have become the killing of children. This is why I say, A Promise to Our Children,

I will not be a part of the killing
of any child,
no matter how lofty the reason.
Not my neighbor's child. Not my child.
Not the enemy's child.
Not by bomb. Not by bullet.
Not by looking the other way.
I will be the power that is peace.

Spoken out loud, these words have a way of traveling out, taking form, and becoming the change our world needs. They also travel in. Through repetition of the Promise, I learn that I can speak out against war---serial wars, perpetual wars, the next war. I can learn and practice nonviolent solutions to conflict. I can choose a peaceful livelihood and encourage my children to do the same. I can insist that my tax dollars go to feed and house the desperate. I can follow spiritual leaders whose message is peace: Isaiah, Lao Tzu, Buddha, Jesus, Mohammad, Gandhi, Badshah Kahn, M. L. King, Dorothy Day, Rabbi Abraham Heschel, Peace Pilgrim, Thich Nhat Hanh, Dalai Lama, Desmond Tutu.

Through repetition of the Promise, I learn that the place love goes deepest---the love we each have for our own child---is the meeting place. I see that only when your child is safe in the world, will my child be safe.

COMMENTARY continue

I hope you will join me in saying out loud, A Promise to Our Children. The words are simple. They are also familiar. Our hearts have been saying them all along.

I will not be part of the killing
of any child...

24

Walter Wink (1935-2012) was an American, Christian theologian, educator and author. The following episode, which took place during the Civil Rights movement in the 1960's, is reported in his book, *Jesus and Nonviolence, A Third Way*.

One evening, during the turbulent weeks when Selma, Alabama, was the focal point of civil rights struggle, the large crowd of black and white activists standing outside the Ebenezer Baptist Church was electrified by the sudden arrival of a black funeral home operator from Montgomery. He reported that a group of Black students demonstrating near the capitol that afternoon had been surrounded by police on horseback, all escape barred, and cynically commanded to disperse or take the consequences. Then the mounted police waded into the students and beat them at will. Police prevented ambulances from reaching the injured for two hours. Our informant was the driver of one of those ambulances, and he had driven straight to Selma to tell us about it.

The crowd outside the church seethed with rage. Cries went up. "Let's march!" Behind us, across the street, stood, rank on rank, the Alabama State Troopers and the local police forces of Sheriff Jim Clark. The situation was explosive. A young Black minister stepped to the microphone and said, "It's time we sang a song." He opened with the line, "Do you love Martin King?" to which those who knew the song responded, "Certainly, Lord!" "Do you love Martin King?" "Certainly, certainly, certainly Lord!" Right through the chain of command of the Southern Christian Leadership Conference he went, the crowd each time echoing, warming to the song. "Certainly, certainly, certainly Lord!" Without warning he sang out, "Do you love Jim Clark?" the sheriff?! "Cer..certainly, Lord" came the stunned, halting reply. "Do you love Jim Clark?" "Certainly, Lord" –it was stronger this time. "Do you love Jim Clark?" Now the point had sunk in…"Certainly, certainly, certainly Lord!"

24 continue

Rev. James Bevel then took the mike. We are not just fighting for our rights, he said, but for the good of the whole society. "It's not enough to defeat Jim Clark – do you hear me Jim? – we want you converted. We cannot win by hating our oppressors. We have to love them into changing."

Jim Clark did change. When the voter registration drive in Selma was concluded, Jim Clark realized that he could not be re-elected without the Black vote, so he began courting Black voters. Later he even confessed, and I believe sincerely, that he had been wrong in his bias against Blacks.

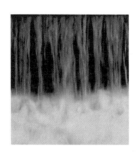

COMMENTARY

"It's time we sang a song."

How weak those words from the young minister must have sounded to that angry crowd in front of the Ebenezer Baptist Church. And when he sang out, "Do you love Martin King?," it's a wonder anyone knew what to make of it. But a few folks recognized the old Gospel hymn and called back, "Certainly, Lord. Certainly." And the crowd soon caught on to the back and forth rhythm and, name after name, sang "Certainly, Lord. Certainly." And the mood of anger gave way to peace.

Then, sudden as a spit in the face, came the stumbling block name, "Jim Clark." But the momentum of the song carried them through and they heard themselves singing, "Certainly, Lord, Certainly."

What is it that happens when the word "love" is given a name and sung? Does it travel in the air, take on light, enter us? By whatever magic, it's the hated name---the owned politician, the bully, war monger, terrorist, slum lord, hard to like boss/neighbor/relative---that makes the song and us. "Certainly, Lord, Certainly."

There is a name that is a stumbling block for me, and not only me. I need to go to the church I call home and step before the congregation and say, "It's time we sang a song."

25

Once a week for 16 years, I visited my friend Bill VanRy in his home. Our excuse for getting together was exercise. Bill, then in his 80's and 90's, was a professional trainer and proof of a lifetime of fitness. He called it, "long-term practice."

Each session ended with conversation over coffee. Although Bill had only an eighth-grade education, he'd read a library of books and was a natural philosopher. His vocabulary was fresh, could startle, and often came from an earlier era: prevaricate, strapping, Holy Ghost, jalopy, trousers, gumption.

Bill had no interest in small talk, so we risked ideas and feeling and mystery. Much of it was God talk. We were safe with one another, and often found ourselves saying what we didn't know we knew.

Occasionally, we touched on the preciousness of our friendship, and rarer, a confidence. During a careful conversation about the challenges of marriage, I said, "Bill, I've got the answer. Magnanimity!"

"I like the sound of that," he said. "What does it mean?"

"I'm not sure."

"Let's not look it up," he said. "It'll come to us."

Not too often, maybe three or four times a year, just as I was going out the door, Bill would call out, "Remember: Magnanimity! Magnanimity!"

COMMENTARY

The discomfort Bill and I confessed is a common one---the daily challenge of getting along with the person we are closest to. Love, commitment, faithfulness, these served us, but still we stumbled.

The word "magnanimity" held promise. What we were looking for was a wide stance.

Shortly after Bill died, I read *The Novice*, a novel by peacemaker Thich Nhat Hanh. Based on a true story, it takes place in 16th century Vietnam. In it, a young woman, Kinh Tam, disguises herself as a man so she can become a Buddhist monk.

Kinh Tam is radiant and gifted and seen by her fellow monks as compassion itself. When they discover that Kinh's a woman, their inspired solution is to invite her to start the first Zen monastery for women.

Late in the story, Kinh takes on, "The Practice of Magnanimity." When I read this, I stopped. "Magnanimity. A practice!" Bill may have heard me.

Kinh Tam describes magnanimity as inclusiveness---a loving kindness, especially to those who frustrate or may injure us, those who, like ourselves, are subject to ignorance and unskillful behavior.

The definition had come.

Kinh Tam also offered an analogy, *"When you pour salt in the palm of your hand and then put it into a cup of water, the water becomes undrinkable. But if you put the same handful of salt into a flowing river, it affects the river and your ability to drink it not at all."*

Magnanimity. It's the answer.

26

Shulamith Hareven (1930-2003) was one of Israel's most revered writers. In 1988, she wrote an essay about Israel's need to sign accords with her Arab neighbors. It is titled, "Without Love," and begins with this anecdote.

A cab driver advises: "Lady, you take it from me: What we gotta do is grab those Arabs, and get a big stick, and hit them over the head but good---hit 'em and hit 'em until they quit hating us."

COMMENTARY

Reading Hareven's anecdote, I can't help but smile. How ridiculous, to believe someone will stop hating us if we keep hitting them over the head! But such logic and such words are common. I hear them every day. They're ridiculous, but not funny.

Behind the bluntness of the driver's words, I hear something wistful, something that wants to be said and is common to all peoples: If only they knew us. We're a good, loveable people.

We aren't told if the "Lady" in the story, who may have been Hareven, said anything back to the driver. If I were the one in the back seat, what would I say? From the safe distance of a reader, I know what I would like to say: *Friend, we don't need to get a big stick. We just need to put down the one already in our hand, and be the one willing to take the last hit.*

27

On *The Daily Show*, October. 10, 2013, host Jon Stewart interviewed Malala Yousafzai, a 16-year- old Pakistani girl who had been shot in the head by a Taliban assassin because of her outspoken advocacy for the education of girls. Malala, unconscious and in critical condition, was flown from her village to London for treatment. She recuperated and was asked to tell her story. *Time* magazine featured her as "one of the 100 most influential people in the world," and she was co-recipient of the 2014 Nobel Prize for Peace.

Jon Stewart: **When did you realize the Taliban had made you a target?**

Malala: **When in 2012, I was with my father, and someone came and she told us, "Have you seen Google and searched your name? The Taliban has targeted you."**

I just could not believe it, and I said, "No it's not true." And even after we saw it, I was not worried, I was worried about my father. Because I did not think the Talib was that cruel that they would kill a child.

I was 14 at the time. But later on I started thinking about that, and I used to think that the Talib would come and he would just kill me. But then I thought, "What would you do, Malala?" And I think to myself, "Malala, just take a shoe and hit him."

But then I said: "If you hit a Talib with your shoe, then there would be no difference between you and the Talib. You must not treat others with cruelty and that harshly. You must fight others, but through peace and dialogue and education. Then I tell him that what they are trying to do is wrong. That education is a basic right. That you would want education for your children as well.

"That is what I want to tell you. Now do what you want."

COMMENTARY

As I watch Malala tell her story, and take in her smile, her warmth, her modesty, her delight, I find myself smiling. Hers is the borderless light of goodness. I find it hard to remember she is not a child, but a young woman.

It was such a small choice, the putting down of a shoe. But with it, Malala showed us how to be done with violence: dismiss the fantasy of it.

The word "hero" applies here. She is honest, speaks out, and is not afraid to die.

To the terrorist who would come, she planned to appeal to his love for his own daughter. "...you would want education for your children as well." But the two young men who jumped aboard her school bus with guns left no time for words. "Who is Malala?" they asked, then shot her in the head.

Malala survived, and knew what to do with the gift of more life. She told her story. It's about the new beginning that comes with putting down a shoe, or a revolver, or the fear that we will be smaller if someone else becomes larger.

As I listen to Malala, I hear all our mothers and sisters and daughters saying: as women, we accept responsibility for bringing new life into the world. As men, you need to accept responsibly for not taking life.

28

Judith Malina (1926 -2015) was an actor, activist, co-founder of The Living Theater in New York, and an inductee to the Theater Hall of Fame. In 2006, Romy Ashby interviewed her for *Goodie Magazine*. In this excerpt from that interview, Malina, 80, tells about a pivotal event in her life.

When I was about 12, I went to the Beacon Theatre (in NY City) and saw a movie called Nurse Edith Cavell (1939) starring Anna Neagle. It was based on a real story about a nurse in WWI who was working the ambulance corps on the battle fields. And she refused not to pick up any wounded man, whether he was a German or English or Belgian or American. She would simply not distinguish. And once a soldier was cured, she would send him back to his lines. One day she was arrested and sentenced to death for treason. The Germans took her out and shot her.

Hollywood added its glamour by showing us the burial of Edith Cavell in England with a scene of the choir singing, coming in for a close up, of Anna Neagle's face juxtaposed with the magnificence of the cathedral as she recited, in her magnificent British accent, lines that Edith Cavell actually wrote on the morning of her death in her cell:

> *Standing as I am before God and eternity, I realize that patriotism is not enough. I must have no hatred or bitterness toward anyone.*

And I thought, I've finally heard something! It's absolutely true and it's so clear now to me!

I ran home to my rabbinical father who was trying to make people aware of what the Nazis were doing to the Jews, and I said, "Papa, I just learned the most important thing! I've learned the most incredible thing in the world!" I said: "Papa, we must not hate the Nazis."

And, oh! I've been in trouble from that day to this. I've been in jail in 12 different countries, only because I believe that. Not for anything I'm ashamed of. I've done plenty of things I'm ashamed of, but I never got busted for them. I got busted for believing this: that I must have no hatred or bitterness toward anyone. Nazis, Germans, Iranians, Al Qaeda.

COMMENTARY

...Patriotism is not enough. I must have no hatred or bitterness toward anyone.

These words struck young Judith Malina as truth, as something written in the heart. And they became for her a message to be lived and shouted. And like most peace messages, before anything else, it disturbed. "Papa, we must not hate the Nazis."

Judith became a prophetic, fiery original---actor, pacifist, poet, anarchist, activist. Her home was New York City, but she and husband Julian Beck traveled the world performing experimental theater, often in the streets and behind prison bars. They were their message: nonviolent revolution.

I demand everything---total love, an end to all forms of violence and cruelty such as money, hunger, prisons, people doing work they hate. I demand it now.

-Judith Malina, New York Times interview, 1968

Judith's life was changed by the example and words of nurse Edith Caville. My life, among so many others, has been changed by the example of Judith Malina. Of all the lovely, charged words she spoke, I look to four from the 1968 Living Theater production of "Paradise Now." They are commissioning words. She was standing on stage naked.

Be the heart. Act.

29

Cornel Pewewardy (Comanche-Kiowa), former Professor and Director of Indigenous Nations Studies at Portland State University in Oregon, shared this personal story at a Peace Symposium in 2013.

My father was a World War II veteran who had been captured and held by the Germans as a prisoner of war. When I asked him what it was like to be a POW, he said, "It wasn't so bad. I'd been a prisoner of war before." He was referring to being taken from his home on a reservation at a young age and forced, along with so many other Native American children, to attend "Indian School" until he finished high school.

He told me he learned four things at that school: *individualism, materialism, competition, and Euro-Centrism.*

COMMENTARY

One morning years ago, I drove by a pasture where cows were grazing and saw that a herd of elk were moving through that same field. There were 30 or more, some with antlers, and they were large and athletic and magnificent. I stopped the car to watch. When the elk came to the far fence, one after another, gracefully, effortlessly, they leapt over. Some of the cows lifted their heads, as if they'd heard a familiar but distant sound, then put their noses back to the ground.

Hearing Pewewardy's story about his father, reminded me of that elk moment and the thought I had as I drove away, "Which am I, the head-down cow, or the elk who jumps the fence?"

The schools I attended as an Anglo boy in Nebraska taught the same four lessons as the Indian School, I just wasn't aware of being a prisoner.

Pewewardy's father leapt the four-sided fence meant to keep him in and tame him. I intend to leap it too:

* Instead of individualism, I want an identity based on belonging, and usefulness.
* Instead of materialism, I want to excel at giving with both hands.
* Instead of competition, I want to arrive together today, with no one left behind.
* Instead of Euro-Centrism, I want to learn about each people, beginning with the First People.

30

One evening in 1982, writer Isaac Bashevis Singer gave a reading at Memorial Hall on the Harvard campus in Cambridge, Massachusetts. He was 81 years old.

The auditorium was packed to hear this Nobel Prize winner, and we stood and applauded as he walked across the stage to the podium. He wore the traditional black suit and white shirt of a man of letters. He was small and impish, and his white hair shone.

"Tonight," he said, "I'm going to read two short stories. The first you may know, but the second hasn't been published and, for me, is unusual. It has a moral."

We listened. The silence of our attention held him and seemed to swell as he paused to take a sip of water and turn a page.

When he'd finished and stood through the ovation, he said, "Ladies and gentlemen, ask me any question you feel like asking. If I know the answer, I vill answer you, and if I don't know the answer I vill answer you anyhow." A woman near the front stood and asked, "Mr. Singer, would you please tell us the moral of the second story."

"The moral is, if you can't be a good Jew, act like one!"

COMMENTARY

Singer's words are spiritually playful and ring true whatever your religion. It's not purity of intent or lack of it that counts, it's what we do.

> Singer says: *When you read the Bible it never tells you what a person thought.*
> *It's always what he or she did.*

When I offer someone a ride to the doctor, I may feel coerced or half-hearted or put-out. When I send an anonymous check, I may hope that I'll be found out. When I stand listening to someone in the grocery aisle who lives alone and can't stop talking, my legs may ache, and I may feel impatient or distracted or like screaming. But the person receiving my performance knows only the performance.

> Singer says: *When you are really hungry you don't look for the biography of the baker.*

If you can't be a good Jew...good Christian...good Muslim...citizen... spouse...parent...next door neighbor...peacemaker, then act like one!

Actions reach out, but they also reach in. We become what we practice.

31

In 1948, Costa Rica had a revolution and abolished its military. The leader of that revolution, Jose Figueres, became President. Today, his daughter, Christiana Figueres, heads the U.N. Framework Convention on Climate Change.

Forty years ago, when Christiana finished college, she chose to go into the Talamanca Mountains of Costa Rica to do volunteer work with the Bribri - an indigenous tribe who were isolated and living a Stone Age existence.

She took a camera with her to document the Bribri's lives, and discovered that they loved to see photographs of themselves. So, every few months, she trekked out of the mountains by foot and by donkey to get the pictures developed.

Returning from one of those trips, Christiana also brought with her a postcard she'd received showing New York City at night. "I wanted to see how *they* would interpret it," she said. "So I just showed them the photograph, and asked, 'What is this?'"

These were primitive people who lived with no running water or electricity. They had no concept of what a lit city was. The only light they had ever seen at night was the stars.

Looking at the postcard, they said, "Ah. All the little stars of heaven in rows."

COMMENTARY

You and I are children of a dark century. The names "Auschwitz" and "Hiroshima" indict us. We feel our complicity and fear more of the same.

American historian Kent D. Shifferd studied the 20th century and saw its darkness. But he noticed something else: during that same 100 years, humanity created new institutions and endeavors and movements which were life affirming and were expanding. Like the Bribri, he saw that all the scattered lights had come near and arranged themselves in rows against the night. Shifferd called these rows of lights, Trends. He saw,

* Institutions where nations gather to prevent war through negotiation

(e.g., The United Nations, European Union, Organization of American States)

* Laws & treaties which have been adopted and accepted by international agreement

(e.g., Nuclear Test Ban Treaty, Chemical Weapons Convention, Mine Ban Treaty)

* The history, number and success of nonviolent revolutions

(e.g., India's independence, U.S. Civil Rights Movement, South Africa, the Philippines)

* Proliferation of humanitarian, nongovernment organizations (NGOs)

(e.g., Rotary International, Doctors Without Borders, Mercy Corps, Human Rights Watch)

* Transformative social changes

(e.g., Women's Rights, Environmental Movement, religious pluralism, internet web)

* Creation of unarmed, citizen-based peacekeeping forces

(e.g., Nonviolent PeaceForce, Peace Brigades International, Code Pink)

Shifferd, with the help of peace scholar Patrick Hiller, identified 28 *Trends*. And he saw that, through their moral affinity, these Trends converge to form a *Global Peace System*. This System, real and bright as a row of stars, is replacing the old, dark, military industrial system.

The *Global Peace System* is history become news. *Hopeful* news.

32

Don Eaton, a singer and musician, told this story at a gathering of United Church of Christ friends in Portland, Oregon:

Years ago, I was asked to do an anti-drug program at a large high school. It was held in the auditorium with about 1,200 students.

I sang and gave my message, and invited students to send up requests for songs or any questions they had. Printed on the front of one of the notes was, "Ask me to stand up," signed, "Kevin."

So I called his name and he stood and the spotlight found him. Then, he stood on his chair. "Don," he said, "please read my note." I unfolded the note and read:

"My name is Kevin and I'm a student here. I don't care if you are tall or short, skinny or fat. I don't care if you are black or yellow or red or brown or white.

"I don't care if you are a nerd, jock or cheerleader.

"I don't care if you are attracted to boys or girls.

"I don't care if you are a straight-A student or flunking.

"You are safe with me."

Standing on his chair in the spotlight, Kevin then held out his arms in a gesture of open welcome and vulnerability.

"I just thought you should know," he said. "No sarcasm here. No nicknames. No put downs. No pressure to be cool.

"You are *safe* with me."

COMMENTARY

You and I know what it is to be excluded: not invited, not needed, made invisible. We also know what it is to exclude: to turn from the contamination of newcomers, the one with the wrong socks, the misfits, the NOKD (Not Our Kind Dear).

What we want is the wall of backs to open when we approach. We want to know the easy laughter, careless stance, the heedlessness, the free pass of popularity.

Kevin offers a new beginning. He erases the hateful line between inside and outside. Everyone is just here, standing too close to size one another up or down. Each person his or her own unlikely, stunning, not-yet-there self.

I don't know how many students joined Kevin after the program. Maybe the miracle happened and one-by-one they came and stood around him, and he stepped down from his chair. But maybe no one gathered, each one too embarrassed, too unsure to admit the size of his or her need.

But Kevin's invitation stands. And you and I, long past high school, know that to join him is to *become* him: to stand up, arms open, hearts exposed, and say out loud, "You are *safe* with me."

33

Phillip Berrigan (1923 – 2002) served in the U.S. Army in Germany during WWII. Following a battlefield commission, he commanded troops as an artillery and infantry officer. After the war, he became a Catholic priest in the Society of St. Joseph.

During the Vietnam War, Berrigan founded the Catholic Peace Fellowship and led draft board raids which helped mobilize American opposition to that war. In 1970, he married former nun Elizabeth McAlister and was excommunicated from the Church. He and his wife founded Jonas House---a community to support resistance to war. He paid with 11 years in jails and prisons.

Berrigan dedicated his life to active moral opposition to what he called "the American Empire." He believed that war, racism, and poverty were inseparable strands of a corrupt economic system.

In *The Autobiography of Philip Berrigan*, he shares this story:

In my own case, I remember May 1945, when I came close to shooting two German prisoners of war who happened to be Waffen SS, Hitler's elite bodyguard troops. They stared at us arrogantly and hatefully and cursed us Americans in German as we slowly passed them at a railroad siding, a few days after the German surrender in May 1945. They were unarmed, I was armed, an officer of the victorious American Army---and I could hardly stomach their hatred and hostility. I very nearly shot them, knowing at the time that if I had, a mere tap on the wrist would result as punishment. They were SS scum, unworthy to live. And I was a victor, with the right to shoot them or let them live.

I have come from that level of brutalization as a young infantry officer to today and the certainty that my relationship to an enemy is precisely my relationship to God. It makes no difference if the enemy has truly harmed me or attempted to kill me---or if the government has picked my enemy---a Communist, Arab, Cuban, North Korean, Libyan. No difference whatsoever. My enemy might be artificial or real---he or she still bears the image of God and what I do to them I do to God.

COMMENTARY

My relationship to an enemy is precisely my relationship to God. When I first read those words, I was stunned, and continue to be.

Imagine, to hate another, even one wearing the black boots and peaked cap of the Waffen SS, is to hate God. To spit, to slap, to strike another is to strike God. To sneer is to sneer in the face of God. To kill another is to cause in God the hollowing, lasting pain a parent feels at the death of his or her own child.

What a terrible power for us to have---to bring through our choices suffering, not joy, to God.

Berrigan's theology is one of intimacy, founded in the One he followed. "As I am in the father and the father in me," said Jesus, "so are you in me and I in you." God's being is there in our neighbor, the stranger, the least among us, and in our enemy. This mutual indwelling is a mystery. Perhaps only through risking intimacy can it be seen.

To crucify anyone is to crucify the One.

34

Once upon a time there was a small village at the foot of a mountain. High up, it was said, there lived a hermit---an old woman wise and good.

Some of the people in the village believed this sage existed; others weren't so sure.

A group of young people decided to go and see for themselves. They started early one morning. The path was steep and the forest shadowed. They laughed as they linked hands to cross a rushing stream. They picked tiny blue flowers. They entered glades of soft, yellow light. Deer, fox and many small eyes watched them, and birds announced their coming.

As they neared the mountain top, they smelled chimney smoke, then saw an old woman standing on the path ahead. She motioned to them. "Come. I've been waiting for you."

The young people sat on the grass in front of her hut, and the woman brought tea. She asked their names, and carefully repeated them back: Sarah, Ishmael, Kim… She asked about their families, what they read in school, what songs they sang, and where they dreamed of going.

They found it easy to talk with her and felt happy.

When the shadows lengthened and the air turned cool, the woman said, "You need to get down before dark."

"But we haven't asked what we came to ask," Kim said

"Oh?"

"We want to know," Kim said, "what it is that makes you wise and good?"

The old woman laughed. "That's easy. I used to be me. Now I am you."

COMMENTARY

It is the way of boys and girls who live in valleys to seek out the one who lives on the mountain top. On that high ground, the young people in the story meet an old woman who tells them what every wise person knows: separation is an illusion. And she knows how to say it: "I used to be me. Now I am you."

The story ends there, and like the young people heading down the mountain, I am left to think about it. I know that each of us is part of an immense, intricate, intimate, interdependent whole. I believe we arrive at the joy of this truth when we lose ourselves in caring for one another, but I forget and need reminding, lots of reminding.

> *We are the sum of our relationships.*
>
> -Martin Buber

> *Each of us, helplessly and forever contains the other---*
> *male in female, female in male, white in black and*
> *black in white.*
>
> -James Baldwin, "The Price of the Ticket"

> *It is a fact that all the elementary particles can be trans*
> *formed into one another.*
>
> -Werner Heisenberg

At the bottom of the mountain, I imagine the young people arriving home, and their excited telling of what they'd learned from the wise woman: "I used to be me. Now I am you." I see their mothers smiling. How deeply mothers know this.

You and I are no more separate from one another than the mountain is from the valley. The one makes the other.

35

The Tao Te Ching (The Way) is an ancient Chinese wisdom text dating from 600 BCE. It is attributed to Lao Tzu, a mysterious wandering monk. He taught that humankind is at home in the universe and is meant to live in harmony with it. He emphasized the creative power of stillness, and dismissed assertive action as inefficient. "The way to do," he said, "is to be."

The text consists of 81 entries. They are numbered, written in verse, and most are brief enough to fit on a single page. Number *78* illustrates wisdom through the example of the way of water.

*Nothing in the world
is as soft and yielding as water.
Yet for dissolving the hard and inflexible,
nothing can surpass it.*

*The soft overcomes the hard,
The gentle overcomes the rigid.
Everyone knows this is true,
but few can put it into practice.*

… True words seem paradoxical.

-from #78, Tao Te Ching

translated by Stephen Mitchell

COMMENTARY

I turn to *The Tao* for the peace I find in its words, and its confirmation of the wisdom of nonviolence. It assures me that gentleness is folded into creation, is at work, and will prevail.

Like water, it is supple and seeks the lowest place.

The Tao also invites me to look and read for myself creation's open page. I look at the faces of children, their gladness, and see each one as the one we have been waiting for. I look at summer clouds, how they build and brighten, then are gone, and am relieved of my certainties. I look at the sprout in the warming compost, and know that life gives on only to more life. I look at the full moon, and wonder what light I reflect.

I look at a chalk colored canyon and stream below, and see that,

> *The soft overcomes the hard.*
> *The gentle overcomes the rigid.*

—#78

36

I Vow

To be a more peaceful presence
shoulders down, eyes soft,
open to what comes next

To listen in
to set aside quiet time
to hear what I otherwise would not hear, and most need

To be the first to be vulnerable
to smile, to say "I'm sorry," to extend an invitation, to ask for
help

To hurry less
trusting there is time enough

To keep a low, gentle voice
I needn't insist
I could be wrong

To send peaceful thoughts
to those who seem sad, anxious, despairing, alone
and those who irk, threaten, injure, oppress

To live simply
knowing how much is enough

To practice forgiveness
moving on, wishing the other person well

To walk softly on the earth
with reverence, with reverence

To love my enemy
to risk injury rather than to injure
to trust the Divine is there in disguise

COMMENTARY

Several years ago, I called on Rabbi Aryeh Hirschfield in Portland, Oregon, to invite him and his congregation to participate in *Fields of Peace*---an interfaith network of congregations committed to emphasizing the message of peace and nonviolence.

Rabbi Aryeh and I talked for most of the afternoon. We had each found a friend. Although he expressed interest in *Fields*, he asked me to come back in a week. When I returned, he explained that he'd needed to take his own vow of nonviolence before accepting my invitation. I confessed that I had yet to take a formal vow.

To take a vow of nonviolence in our culture, which avows "the survival of the fittest," is to declare that,

Survival is the second law of life.
The first is that we are all one.

-Joseph Campbell

I looked for the right vow. I wanted something I could look to each morning. Finally, I drafted my own list of ten. They are a beginning. The most important words are the first two: I Vow.

As I made my list, I kept in mind Rabbi Aryeh's quoting Rabbi Abraham Heshel: "To remain tender in the midst of inward panic."

37

For many years, American writer Madeleine L'Engle (1918 – 2007) was writer-in-residence at the Cathedral of St. John the Divine in New York City. In this piece, she recalls a worship service she attended there.

A decade or so ago one evening during Lent,…I listened to the Reverend Canon Edward West talk about the peace we seek, and use the rather unexpected metaphor of a subway.

Most of us in the audience that night rode the subway to the Cathedral. He pointed out to us that if we looked at the people riding in the same car with us, most of them would look as though nobody loved them. And that, alas, was largely true.

Then he told us that if we would concentrate inconspicuously on one person, affirming silently that this person was beloved and, no matter what the circumstances, could be peace, we might see a difference. Peace is not always something you "do;" it is a gift you can give.

The next time I rode the subway I glanced at a woman in the corner, hunched over, hands clenched, an expression of resigned endurance on her face. So, without looking at her, I began to try to send loving peace to her.

I didn't move. I didn't stare at her. I simply followed Canon West's suggestion, and to my wonder she began to relax. Her hands unclenched; her body relaxed; the lines of anxiety left her face. It was a moment for me of great gratitude, and a peace that spread out and filled me too.

….We can be vehicles of peace, and our own peace will be thereby deepened.

COMMENTARY

The practice L'Engle suggests is intriguing. I give it a try.

In a restaurant one evening with my wife and son, I see an elderly man alone at a table. He doesn't look up when the waiter fills his water glass. He's intent on his plate. I peg him as a widower who's tired of what he can fix for himself, and the sight of a kitchen table with one placemat.

Without looking over, I send him peace---a little cloud from my chest to his. I imagine it disappearing into him like fog. And he looks up, as if a breeze has just entered the room.

Since then, when I remember, which isn't very often, I send a little cloud.... To a woman at a check-out stand dumping out her purse to find her food stamps....To a couple having words on the sidewalk....To a young man sitting next to me in a waiting room whose right leg is bouncing.....To the driver of a pick-up truck riding the bumper of my car.

It's hard to tell. The boy's leg did stop bouncing. The truck slid back a bit. Maybe there is a frequency or beam which we, so taken by words, have forgotten how to use.

Whether I'm feeling peaceful or not, I find I've got peace to send to out.

38

On January 1, 1953, a woman walked out the door of her house in Pasadena, California, to begin a pilgrimage. She called it, *a gentle journey of prayer and example*. Her mission was to help bring about peace in the world by helping others find inner peace. As she stepped out, she gave herself a new name, *Peace Pilgrim*, and made a vow:

I will walk until given shelter and fast until given food, remaining a wanderer until humankind has learned the way of peace.

She wore slacks, and a navy-blue tunic with white letters on the front: *Peace Pilgrim*. Her only possessions were a comb, toothbrush, pen, and a few pamphlets with her pilgrimage message:

This is the way to peace:
Overcome evil with good, falsehood with truth, hatred with love.

Peace Pilgrim walked through every state of the union, all the provinces of Canada, and a bit of Mexico. Most days she covered 25 miles. She would not accept a ride, or money. Most days she was offered more food than she needed, and slept equally well at night in a field or someone's guest bedroom. In 28 years on the road, she was never ill, never even had a cold.

Peace Pilgrim was often interviewed on radio and television, and invited to preach at churches, and talk at schools and universities. When asked, "What results have you seen from all your pilgrim-ing?" She replied, *It never occurred to me to ask to seek results. I leave the results in God's hands.*

Peace Pilgrim died in 1981. Her memorial is that we remember her message:

Overcome evil with good, falsehood with truth, hatred with love.

COMMENTARY

What was it that enabled Peace Pilgrim to live a life of such originality and courage and purpose? I want to know the story behind the story so that I too might step out and live a larger life. Reading her story, perhaps that's what we all want to know.

One evening, she tells us, she went for a walk in the woods near her house. When it became dark, she continued on. She thought about her life, its direction and depth, how she fit the mold of what was expected, but not the larger promise within her. At one point she came to a moonlit glade and stopped. "I felt a complete willingness, without any reservations, to give my life...to dedicate my life to service. I prayed, 'Please use me!'"

Then, patiently, over a period of years, she set about changing her life.

* *She gave up her morning cup of coffee and other habits that hindered her health and strength. "You don't stop bad habits gradually. You just stop."*

* *She stopped judging others. "There's only one person you can change, and it's yourself."*

* *She gave up trivial entertainments and unnecessary comforts, and replaced them by spending time with people in need.*

* *She purified her thoughts. "If you realized how powerful your thoughts are, you would never think a negative thought." "I fear nothing, and expect only good."*

* *She simplified her material possessions. "I could no longer accept more than I needed while others in the world have less than they need. This brought my life down to need level. Now, what I want and what I need are exactly the same."*

* *She stopped worrying. "You worry, you agonize over the past which you should have forgotten long ago, or , you're apprehensive over the future which hasn't even come yet. We tend to skim right over the present time. Since this is the only moment that anyone can live, if you don't live it, you never really get around to living at all. But if you do live this present moment, you tend not to worry."*

Commentary continue

Only then, after this long, thorough, disciplined interior journey, did she step out her front door and become Peace Pilgrim. To us, she says, "You have a part in the scheme of things. What that part is, you can know only from within yourself. You can seek it in receptive silence. There is a guidance which comes from within to all who will listen."

39

I belong to a small fanatical sect. We believe that current ways of carrying on world affairs are malignant. We believe that armies, and the kind of international dealings based on armed might, will be self-perpetuating to a certain point---and that point may bring annihilation. Armies are the result of obsolete ways---just as gibbets are, and as thumb-screws are, and leper windows.

William Stafford, poet

Not national security. Human security.

Jody Williams, Nobel Peace Prize Laureate

The bomb (atom) was the absolute weapon in this sense: What human beings, no matter how depraved, would never have had the moral capacity to do over time and personally---with ice picks---they would do now with nary a second thought---in a second.

James Carroll, novelist and historian

What unbearable suffering there is in the world today, all around us, in mental hospitals, in prisons as well as in war, and we know little more about them than the Germans claimed to know of the atrocities committed during the Holocaust in Europe.

Dorothy Day, peace activist and founder of The Catholic Worker

The most basic way in which all men may be divided is between those who believe that war is unnecessary and those who believe that war is inevitable; between those to whom the sword is the symbol of honor and those to whom seeking to convert swords into plowshares is the only way to keep our civilization from disaster.

Rabbi Abraham Joshua Heschel

War violates every right of the child.

Graca Machel, Chair, U.N. study, Impact of Armed Conflict on Children

COMMENTARY

Hearing these voices, I am reminded of the Hebrew prophets: Hosea, Isaiah, Jeremiah, Micah. Like those ancients, our contemporary prophets stand in the public square and call out the moral failures of our time and nation, and warn of the consequences to follow. And they refuse to be quiet.

I'm heartened, and alerted, by the number of these voices in just the last century. Many are religious: Tolstoy, Gandhi, Bhad Shah Kahn, Dietrich Bonhoeffer, Dorothy Day, Abraham Heschel, Martin Luther King, Jr., Peace Pilgrim, Thomas Merton, Dalai Lama, Daniel Berrigan, Desmond Tutu, Pema Chodron, Satish Kumar, Thich Nhat Hanh, and The 13 Indigenous Grandmothers. But there are others, including peace scholars, activists, singers, ecologists, novelists, journalists, gadflies, and always, poets.

> *All I have is a voice*
> *To undo the folded lie...*

-from "September 1, 1939", by W.H. Auden

In their voices, I hear authority, impatience, indignation. I trust the price they are willing to pay. And I value their outrage at even one instance of injustice.

I hear their call to us to turn: turn from state sponsored mass murder. From the systems---economic and military---which demand war and our indifference to the devastations of war. Turn from the rule of death.

> *We must love one another or die.*

-from "September 1, 1939," by W.H. Auden

40

Marine Corps Captain Tyler Boudreau commanded a Rifle Company in Iraq in 2004. His portrait was painted by Matt Mitchell as part of a project titled, "100 Faces of War (Portraits & Words of Americans who served in Iraq and Afghanistan)." Boudreau provided this accompanying statement:

A commander must be cautious not to look too closely into his own heart. He might find things that he does not want to---things that could hinder his ability to make hard decisions in the heat of battle.

In thinking about war, there is what I would describe as a mission-to-troop ratio. A commander must believe in both, he must love them both; but ultimately he must love the mission a little more. He must be prepared to sacrifice the lives of his men for the success of the mission.

But what if a commander looks into his heart and finds that ratio has somehow reversed itself? What if he begins to love the troops more than the mission? What does he do? What can he do?

I stumbled upon this very dilemma as an infantry company commander.

From the disparity I witnessed between policies in Washington and our actions in Iraq, an ambivalence formed inside me. It began to grow geometrically, doubling and redoubling itself until I was consumed by it.

Suddenly I looked at the faces of my Marines and I realized my reverence for them had overwhelmed my reverence for the mission. By definition, then, I was unable to command. I resigned my commission. After twelve years of service, I left the Marine Corps.

COMMENTARY

The reality of what Tyler Boudreau experienced in combat in Iraq hit him soon after he returned home. He became anxious, remote from his wife and children, and unable to sleep.

He was debilitated by nightmarish flashbacks---the torn and bloody bodies of a mother and father and two children in a car which had failed to stop at a checkpoint---the names, faces, and stories of the young men he had sent on patrol who lost limbs, and the one who died.

He was struck by the failures of the mission itself---the impossibility of winning the hearts and minds of the people---the fact that they were generating new insurgents faster than they could ever capture, kill, or incarcerate the old ones.

And, Boudreau was confronted by questions of conscience---what did he refuse to know and could have so easily known about the war---what part did his desire for promotion and the power of command play---how could he "support our troops" without supporting the system and institutions that require war?

He asked himself:

> *What is the disparity between what I believe and what I have done?*
> *Between what I'd been telling myself and what my self was yelling back?*

Boudreau arrived at an indictment of the Iraq War, and simultaneously, awakened to the reverence he felt for each man in his Company. He saw that no mission---the occupation of a nation or city or street or roof of a building---was worth the life of even one of his men.

41

Three Taoist Masters meet. Each has lived on a mountain, presided over a temple, trained novices, and known silence. Now they're elders. They decide to retire and live together. They're birds of a feather.

They build a hut in a forest and, once a week, go to the nearby village to trade wisdom for rice and salt, and on holy days, a little wine. The villagers delight in the sages, and surround and ask them questions. The sages just beam and laugh, and soon everybody is laughing.

Years pass, and one of the sages becomes ill. He tells his companions he is near the end, and asks a promise. "When I go, no fuss. Don't wash my face or comb my hair. Don't change my brown robe for the orange. Just pick me up and carry me to the pyre."

When he dies, his companions keep their promise and simply pick up his body and carry it to the proper place by the river. Word spreads, the villagers gather, and the pyre is lit.

Suddenly laughter and more laughter!

The sage had filled his pockets with firecrackers. Pop, Pop, POPPOP-POPPOP…..

COMMENTARY

It was a quiet August afternoon, and I was sitting with my friend Harrison Hoblitzelle (Hob) on the deck of his Vermont home. We were drinking tea, and enjoying the view --- the grass covered slope of his field, the green valley, and beyond, the silent wall of mountians.

Hob, a Dharma teacher, was telling me about his recent trip to France, and the memories it brought of living there when he was a young man. So his question surprised me: *"If you were able to write your own script, how would you like to die?"* I learned later that Hob had been asked that question by the Buddhist magazine *Tricycle*, and his answer published.

I held my tea, and did what Hob taught: I watched my breath --- coming in, and going out.

"Like Gandhi," I answered, "saying God's name. You?"

"Laughing," Hob said, "Laughing."

42

On December 24, 1967, Rev. Martin Luther King, Jr., delivered a "Christmas Sermon on Peace," in his home church in Atlanta, Ebenezer Baptist Church. I think of it as the "Gettysburg Address" of Christian nonviolence. Speaking directly to those who opposed him in the Civil Rights movement, some of whom stood at the back of the sanctuary, King said:

We shall match your capacity to inflict suffering by our capacity to endure suffering. We will meet your physical force with soul force. Do to us what you will and we will still love you...Bomb our homes and threaten our children, and, as difficult as it is, we will still love you. Send your hooded perpetrators of violence into our communities at the midnight hour and drag us out on some wayside road and leave us half dead as you beat us, and we will still love you. But be ye assured that we will wear you down by our capacity to suffer. One day we shall win freedom, but not only for ourselves. We shall so appeal to your heart and conscience that we shall win you in the process, and our victory will be a double victory.

COMMENTARY

I carried this paragraph from King's sermon in my wallet for years. I wanted the fire of those words in me. I wanted what made my voice shake when I read them aloud to keep shaking me. I wanted the courage to stake it all, as King did, on the truth of Jesus' Sermon on the Mount, on that one cup of words.

> *You have heard that it was said, "You shall love your neighbor*
> *and hate your enemy." But I say to you, love our enemies...*
>
> (Matthew 5:4)

It helps me to know that King's courage was not always sure. There was a night, January 27, 1956, when he sat alone at his kitchen table. He couldn't sleep. There'd been death threats to him and his family, and he felt his resolve slipping, his strength weakening. Then, in the stillness of that kitchen, King heard an "inner voice." He heard Jesus say to him to still fight on:

> *He promised never to leave me, never to leave me alone.*
> *No never alone. No never alone. He promised never to leave me,*
> *never to leave me alone.*

King's "Christmas Sermon" was heard, and by the thousands, men, women and children marched through the streets of the South. They marched unarmed and arm-in-arm into the physical hate of police dogs, charging horses, billy clubs, water cannons, uniformed phalanxes, mobs, shouters, rocks, bombs, tear gas, aimed rifles. And their victory was a double victory.

I still carry King's words with me, though no longer folded on a piece of paper. When I preach them, my voice still shakes.

43

Elliot Ackerman served four tours of duty in Iraq and Afghanistan as a Captain in the U.S. Marine Corps. His role in Afghanistan was to train their soldiers and then accompany them on combat missions. In a radio interview with Rachel Martin on National Public Radio (Feb 22, 2015), Ackerman shared this about his experience:

ACKERMAN: There was a commander I advised named Ishaq. And when I worked with Ishaq, you know, we had sort of an operational rhythm. And one of the things we would do is every two weeks, we'd sit down and schedule our missions. And we would look at the calendar and at the map, and I would say, so Ishaq, you know, what do you want to do? Where do you want to head off to? And Ishaq, he'd been working in this same part of Afghanistan for five years, but lived there his whole life. You know, he would point at the map and say, well, you know, Mr. Elliott, we could go up to Mankrate, this one village, and say, you know, there's always good hunting up in Mankrate. So we'd block off four days on the calendar. We would drive a patrol up to Mankrate. Fifty-fifty odds we'd get into a gun fight up there. Then we'd clean up our trucks, you know, rest and refit for a couple of days.

Ishaq and I would be back in his office sitting on the lumpy sofa, sipping chai, smoking cigarettes. And, you know, we'd look at the map and the calendar, and Ishaq would stroke his face. And I'd say, where do you want to go Ishaq?" He'd say we could go to Rahrakure. You know, Mr. Elliot, there's always good hunting in Rahrakure. But the conversation was never, well you know, Mr. Elliot, if we go to Mankrate, and we hit them in Rahrakure, we'll go one big push to Malakshe. We'll get them across the border into Pakistan. The war will be over. I can go back to raising my crops. You and yours can all go to business school or whatever you want to do. And then that's it. I mean, it's just – it wasn't that type of war.

43 continue

…For him, he was the leader of a 700-man strong Afghan militia unit that employed most of his tribe. He had more in common with being a beat cop as we think of it than being a soldier. But I think the important thing to point out, too, is so did I. I never felt that we were going to hit them in one village and then go to the next village and the war would be over. You know, why was I there? And you know, I was there because this job, working in the military, being in special operations, it was my identity. It defined me. And those types of deployments insured my promotion through the ranks. You know, these are the reasons people continue to fight wars.

COMMENTARY

In this interview, Ackerman said what U.S. politicians and generals cannot admit: it doesn't matter who we fight, because it isn't about winning or losing; it's an end in itself. We are in the business of perpetual war. Our economy and our national identity are bound to it.

This is a hard message to hear, but one I believe many of us already know. How could we not? The U.S. maintains 760 military bases in foreign countries. Each year, one-half of the annual U.S. Budget goes to our military. In 2018, the Defense Department will receive $597.1 billion. This is as much as the military spending of the next 9 countries combined.

Elliot Ackerman is now out of the Marine Corps and has become a journalist and novelist. In his novel, *Green on Blue*, a Pashto Commander named Sabir describes the war he and his troops partner in with the Americans as "ghabban." "Ghabban," Sabir says, "is when someone demands money for protection against a threat they create. For this type of war, the Americans don't have a word. The only one that comes near is racket."

Ghabban: when someone demands money for protection against a threat they create.

44

My father was a story teller, and the stories he told were about the people in the town where he grew up, Howells, Nebraska, population 760. This one is about Ernest Folda, the town's only accountant.

Each morning Mr. Folda would arrive at his one-room office above the Firestone Store at exactly 8:15. He would nod to his secretary Mrs. James, hang up his hat and coat, and sit down at his desk. From his right front trouser pocket he'd take out the little key that fit the lock on the wide center drawer of his desk, turn the key, pull out the drawer, look down, then close the drawer, turn the key, put the key back in his pocket, and swivel around in his chair and say, "Good morning Mrs. James."

In the more than 15 years Mrs. James worked for Mr. Folda, this routine never varied. And in all those years, he never said a word about what it was he looked at in that drawer first thing each morning. And because Mr. Folda was the kind of man he was, private and formal, she never asked.

But, as it turned out, Mr. Folda died a year or two before his anticipated retirement, and it was left to Mrs. James to straighten out the office.

On her first day there alone, she said it was some time before she realized that it was now hers to empty out his desk, to which she now had the key.

I imagine it was with trepidation that she sat down in Mr. Folda's chair and turned the key in the lock. And perhaps she paused a moment before pulling the drawer out.

In it, she said, was a single sheet of ledger paper of the kind accountants use. Across the top, in simple block letters, were the words:

Debits on the left.   Credits on the right.

COMMENTARY

Through the years, I heard my father tell the Ernest Folda story a number of times. The one time I asked him if was true, he said, "true enough."

Mr. Folda was on to something: a daily practice that's simple and grounding, and takes only a moment. And is humble. So I decided to try it. But which words, which elementary words?

On a shelf in my church office, there are three spiral notebooks with quotes I've collected over the years. I take one and open it to a middle page, leaving it to chance to deliver the right words, and write down three possibilities:

> *Whatever you have, you scatter with both hands as you go.*
>
> —Tagore

> *The one thing in the world is spontaneous compassion,*
> *justice is a secondary matter.*
>
> -Dostoevsky

> *Stay bewildered in God, and only that.*
>
> -Rumi

Looking at these, lovely as they are, I turn and take down my Bible. I'm a minister. My most elementary instruction ought to come from scripture. The right words are obvious:

Love God	*Love your neighbor*
with all of your heart	*as yourself*

I write this in block letters at the top of a sheet paper and put it in my top desk drawer. But there was another quote in the notebook which has stayed with me, though I didn't write it down. Words I think Jesus would like.

> *I believe in the God of the stumblebum. The waitress with a throbbing tooth.*
>
> -Don Delillo

45

In his classic book, *The Sabbath*, Rabbi Abraham Joshua Heschel (1907-1972), emphasizes the importance of the Fourth Commandment which is the longest and most detailed of the Ten Commandments:

> *Remember the Sabbath day, and keep it holy. Six days you shall labor and do all your work. But the seventh day is a Sabbath to the Lord your God: you shall not do any work---you, your son or your daughter, your male or female slave, your livestock, or the alien resident in your towns. For in six days the Lord made heaven and earth, the sea and all that is in them, but rested the seventh day; therefore the Lord blessed the Sabbath day and consecrated it.*

-Exodus 20:1-17

Heschel writes,

* This is not a lifestyle suggestion. To keep the Sabbath is as important as not lying or stealing or murdering.
* The Sabbath as a day of rest is not for the purpose of recovering one's lost strength and becoming fit for the forthcoming labor. The Sabbath is a day for the sake of life.
* The Sabbath must all be spent in charm, grace, peace, and great love. It is, therefore, a double sin to show anger on the Sabbath. And a sin to be sad. Even mourning is to be interrupted on the Sabbath.
* The Sabbath leads us to a realm of endless peace, or to the beginning of an awareness of what eternity means.
* What we are depends on what the Sabbath is to us.

COMMENTARY

"It would have been enough," is a refrain from a traditional Jewish Passover prayer. It is a way of emphasizing thanks to Yahweh for the series of blessings which led to the liberation of the people of Israel from slavery in Egypt. Using that refrain, I give thanks for Abraham Heschel's many gifts of peace to us in our day.

It would have been enough if Abraham Heschel had only reminded us of the gift of the Sabbath, and had not lifted up the importance of interfaith respect and friendship. He said:

> *The religions of the world are no more self-sufficient, no more independent, no more isolated than individuals or nations... We must choose between interfaith and internihilism.*

It would have been enough if Abraham Heschel had only reminded us of the gift of the Sabbath and the importance of interfaith friendship, and had not spoken out as an activist during the Vietnam War. He said:

> *At this hour, Vietnam is our most urgent, our most disturbing religious problem....*
>
> *All religious duties recede, all rituals are suspended, except one: to save life and relieve pain.....To speak about God and remain silent on Vietnam is blasphemous.*

It would have been enough if Abraham Heschel had only reminded us of the gift of the Sabbath and the importance of interfaith friendship and spoken out as an anti-war activist, and had not prayed these words:

> *O Lord... We are a generation that has lost the capacity for outrage. We must continue to remind ourselves that in a free society all are involved in what some are doing. Some are guilty, all are responsible.*

46

In the spring of 1938, the people of Austria were preparing to vote on the Anschluss, the annexing of their country by Germany. Franz Jagerstatter, a young Austrian farmer with a wife and three daughters, was opposed. "Please keep it to yourself," a friend told him, "you will get into trouble. Play the game." Franz replied, "The game is a lie."

Franz was a sincere Catholic who attended Mass each day in his hometown of St. Radegund. He saw Hitler's regime as evil, and opposed it as a matter of conscience.

Intimidated by the poised military power of Germany, the people of Austria approved the annexation, and soon after Franz received a draft notice from the Army. "If they call me up," he told his wife Francesca, "I will not serve."

Franz's priest, Fr. Furthauer, sent him to meet with their Bishop in Linz. The Bishop told Franz that his "refusal to serve would make little or no difference to the Nazi war machine. However his death---the law demanded capital punishment for those who refused to serve---would bring grave harm to his wife and children."

Franz agonized over his responsibility to his family, and his need to follow his conscience.

In February 1943, Franz received orders to report for military service. He refused, and was arrested and put in military prison. He wrote to his wife, "I am troubled by the fear that you have so much to suffer on my account."

The prison Chaplain urged Franz to relent. "You have no responsibility as a private citizen for the acts and policy of this government. ... you will merely be following orders like millions of other Catholics, including priests and seminarians."

The officers of the military court were moved by the depth of Jagerstatter's convictions. If he would sign the induction papers, they promised he would not have to lift a gun. He would be a medic. "You are good men," Franz told them, "but I cannot do this." The verdict was death by beheading.

Franz Jagerstatter was executed at the Brandenburg Prison at 4 pm on August 9, 1943. In the letter he wrote that day to his family, he said:

> ...And now your husband, son, father, son-in-law and brother-in-law greets you once more before his final journey. The heart of Jesus, the heart of Mary and my heart are one in time and eternity.

COMMENTARY

The first thing I saw as he welcomed me into his apartment was a statue of a man. It was about three feet tall, carved from blonde wood, and stood on a pedestal next to the door. Seeing my interest, he said, "Do you know the story of Franz Jagerstatter?"

So began my visit with Daniel Berrigan, priest, peacemaker, activist, poet, scholar, teacher, jailbird. The meeting was arranged by a mutual friend, and took place in Berrigan's upper west side apartment in Manhattan. He was in his 80's then, vigorous and engaged as ever.

We talked for an hour or so, then took a walk in his neighborhood and stopped for coffee. We shared a passion for peacemaking and poetry. And we were both friends of Jesus.

In the years that followed, I sent him news of my peace work in Oregon, and occasionally received back a note of encouragement. I liked it that he signed as "Daniel."

Our visit was in 2007. Berrigan died in 2016. "Do you know the story of Franz Jagerstatter?" My hero's first words to me were an introduction to one of his heroes. And now, reading Berrigan, I also hear Jagerstatter.

> *I think of the good, decent, peace-loving people I have known by the thousands, and I wonder. How many of them are so afflicted with the wasting disease of normalcy that, even as they declare for peace, their hands reach out with an instinctive spasm in the direction of their loved ones, in the direction of their comforts, their home, their security, their income, their future, their plans---that twenty-year plan of family growth and unity, that fifty-year plan of decent life and honorable natural demise.*
>
> *....We cry peace, peace, and there is no peace. There is no peace because the making of peace is at least as costly as the making of war - at least as exigent, at least as disruptive, at least as liable to bring disgrace and prison and death in its wake.*

Walking me to the subway, Berrigan shared a line from Camus: "Stand somewhere and pay up." They were parting words.

47

Soon after his election as head of the Roman Catholic Church in 2013, Pope Francis visited the Holy Land. While there he invited the Presidents of Israel and Palestine to come to the Vatican and pray with him for peace. This invitation had about it an air of spontaneity, and the simplicity of genius. It was also spiritually audacious.

Within two weeks, President Shimon Peres and President Mahmoud Abbas honored the invitation and came to Rome. It was a striking scene. Three chairs were set out in the Vatican garden, and the Pope sat as friend and bridge between the two heads of state. Their two peoples sharing the same land and shedding blood for 60 years.

It was a lovely June evening. An ensemble played Barber's "adagio for Strings," and birds came and went from the hedges. Faith leaders from around the world offered Jewish, Christian and Muslim prayers. They spoke Italian, English, Arabic and Hebrew. They spoke as children of Abraham and Sarah. They spoke of the one God.

There was also silence.

After the gathering, the three men planted an Olive tree in the garden. Saying goodbye, they embraced, and Peres and Abbas flew back to Jerusalem.

We loaded a great love onto little bodies...

-Yehuda Amichai, Jerusalem poet

COMMENTARY

We don't know what the two Presidents heard as they prayed with the Pope in the Vatican Garden. We do know that to pray is to return to the original garden. There, if our hearts are right, innocence is renewed, the word we most need is given, and we are sent out once again to repair what we can.

Go in peace Mahmoud Abbas and Shimon Peres. May God's goodness awaken you to your own, and to the goodness of your sisters and brothers, for in this world and the one to come, we only have each other.

*   *   *

In the 1950's, it was common for families to take Sunday afternoon drives. My Nebraska family was part of this. On Saturday our black Chevrolet sedan would be washed, and Sunday after church and lunch, we'd head out, leaving our small town streets for gravel roads and the flat sameness of corn fields. Mom and Dad sat in the front with Dad driving, my sister and I in back. These outings were mandatory.

On one of the drives, I remember, we passed the chapel that stood in an open field. It was early autumn, and the tattered yellow stalks hadn't been plowed under yet. The chapel was tiny, like a play house, but it had a steeple. One window was broken, and the white boards weathered to gray. I'd seen it before.

That's the Kline chapel, my Dad said. Years ago the two Kline brothers farmed that land together. One was married and had children, the other was a bachelor. (My sister and I knew the story and could have told it, but we listened, careful not to look at each other.) One night, it occurred to the married brother that his brother had no children to take care of him in his old age. So he'd go down in the middle of the night to the barn and shovel grain from his bin into his brother's bin. About the same time, it occurred to the bachelor that his brother had children to provide for in the years to come. So he'd go down at night and shovel grain from his bin into his brother's. One night in the dark, the two brothers backed into each other.

COMMENTARY continue

When they'd both passed on, Dad said, the children used the wood from the old barn to build that little chapel. It marks the spot.

It was a wholesome story and aimed at us, but my sister and I didn't dismiss it, not entirely.

48

In the aftermath of the horrors of World War II, the question of human rights was raised in the Assembly of the newly formed United Nations:

To what rights is everyone entitled, no matter who they are or where they live, simply because they are a human being?

A prestigious international committee was formed to answer that most basic question. They found 30 human rights recognized by the peoples of the world as inalienable. These became *The Universal Declaration of Human Rights* which was adopted by the UN General Assembly in Paris on December, 10, 1948. Today, all 192 member states are signatories, and it has been translated (Abkhaz to Zulu) into 473 languages.

Here are eight abbreviated Articles from The Declaration:

* *All human beings are born free and equal in dignity and rights.*

* *Everyone has the right to freedom of thought, conscience and religion, and freedom of expression.*

* *Everyone has the right to take part in the governments of their countries, and to choose its leaders.*

* *Everyone has the right to education. Primary education shall be free.*

* *Every adult has the right to marry and have a family, and is entitled to equal rights in marriage, and at its dissolution.*

* *Every adult has the right to work, to free choice of employment, to just and favorable conditions of work, and the right to equal pay for equal work.*

* *Everyone has the right to property, and no one shall be arbitrarily deprived of his or her property.*

* *Everyone has the right to a standard of living adequate for the health and well being of themselves and their family, including food, clothing, housing, medical care.*

COMMENTARY

It was a spring afternoon, sunny, and I had a few hours of free time from a church conference I was attending in Boise, Idaho. The Anne Frank Memorial Park had been recommended, so I headed there. At the entrance was a large tilted tablet. I stopped to see what it said and read it all the way through. I thought, "Why haven't I ever heard of this? I went to public school for twelve years. To college. Traveled around the world. Went to seminary. I'm in my 50's. Why haven't I ever heard of this?"

The Universal Declaration of Human Rights is a landmark in human history. It stands with and evolved from:

> * *The Cyrus Cylinder (539 BC) in which Cyrus the Great freed his slaves and allowed people to choose their own religions.*
> * *The Magna Carta (1215) which gave people new rights and made the King of England subject to the law of the land.*
> * *United States Declaration of Independence (1776) which proclaimed the right to life, liberty and the pursuit of happiness.*

Of the 192 nations who have signed *The Declaration*, there may not be one which fulfills all 30 human rights. What's significant is that they all aspire to. My favorite is Article #25:

> *Everyone has the right to a standard of living adequate for the health and well-being of self and family, including food, clothing, housing and medical care and necessary social services, and the right to security in the event of unemployment, sickness, disability, widowhood, old age or other lack of livelihood in circumstances beyond his or her control.*

What is known in the dignity of every human heart has now been honored and established. We need to put it on large tablets at the entrances to parks, schools, universities, houses of worship, museums, state capitols, and Congress. And at home, read it out loud to our children.

49

Revenge

by Taha Muhammad Ali, translated by Peter Cole,
Yahya Hijazi, Gabriel Lev

At times ... I wish
I could meet in a duel
the man who killed my father
and razed our home,
expelling me
into
a narrow country.
And if he killed me,
I'd rest at last,
and if I were ready--
I would take my revenge!

*

But if it came to light,
when my rival appeared,
that he had a mother
waiting for him,
or a father who'd put
his right hand over
the heart's place in his chest
whenever his son was late
even by just a quarter-hour
for a meeting they'd set--
then I would not kill him,
even if I could.

*

Likewise ... I
would not murder him
if it were soon made clear that he had a brother or sisters

who loved him and constantly longed to see him.
Or if he had a wife to greet him
and children who
couldn't bear his absence
and whom his gifts would thrill.
Or if he had
friends or companions,
neighbors he knew
or allies from prison
or a hospital room,
or classmates from his school ...
asking about him
and sending him regards.

*

But if he turned
out to be on his own--
cut off like a branch from a tree--
without a mother or father,
with neither a brother nor sister,
wifeless, without a child,
and without kin or neighbors or friends,
colleagues or companions,
then I'd add not thing to his pain
within that aloneness--
not the torment of death,
and not the sorrow of passing away.
Instead I'd be content
to ignore him when I passed him by
on the street--as I
convinced myself
that paying him no attention
in itself was a kind of revenge.

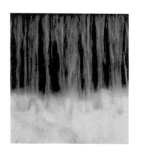

COMMENTARY

Behind this poem and poet, there is a story.

Taha Muhammad Ali was born in the village of Saffuriyya, Galilee. His family had lived there for generations tending orchards and sheep. In 1948, when he was 17, the village was overtaken by Israeli troops. With an hour's notice, all 4,330 inhabitants were forced at gunpoint to leave. Most became refugees in Lebanon and Jordan.

A year later, Taha returned. But Saffuriyya had been bombed to an acreage of gray rubble. Not a wall remained, not a tree. "The air itself," he thought, "has been seized!"

Taha walked on to nearby Nazareth, where he survived by selling souvenirs to Christian pilgrims, and eventually established his own shop. But his ambition was to be a poet. Evenings, he studied classical Arabic, Hebrew and English, world literature, and he wrote. By age 50, Taha's shop was a salon, and he a world-class poet.

"Revenge" was written in 2006, five decades after his father had been killed by an Israeli soldier. It is a personal statement, and a message to the peoples of the Middle East: with empathy and imagination, and time, forgiveness is possible; so is a shared future. There's been enough death.

If I had one sheet of words to stand on the street corner and press into other hands, it would be this poem by Taha Muhammad Ali. He saw something beyond the rubble and walked toward it, and was light enough to call it "revenge."

50

Black Elk (1863 – 1950) was an Oglala Sioux Medicine Man, a *wicasa wakan*---one whose power came from direct contact with the Great Grandfathers.

The Oglala knew themselves to be the Chosen People of Wakan Tanka, the Great Mystery. Their paradise was the Powder River Country of eastern Montana with its big sky and open plain of flowing grass.

When Black Elk was 9, he became gravely ill, and in a coma, experienced a great Vision. He felt himself lifted onto a plain of white clouds. There, in each of the four directions, he saw 48 horses standing. To the east, red sorrel horses with the pure light of understanding and peace. To the west, black horses with the terrible power of the storm. To the north, white horses with endurance, health and wisdom. And to the south, yellow buckskin horses with innocence and the promise of renewed life. Then, he saw the Grandfathers motioning him to their tipi. This Vision, they said, was given to him to save his people from the onslaught of the whites, the Wasichu. The vision ended with him standing on Harney Peak with a view of the entire world.

In the decade following his Vision, Black Elk saw the lands of his people overcome by the Wasichu, and the buffalo gone. He saw his warrior people defeated by the U.S. Army, and betrayed by a treaty. He saw his proud people impoverished, captive, diseased, and dying.

To learn the "secret" of the Wasichu, Black Elk joined Bill Cody's Wild West Show and traveled across "the great water" to London and Paris. He found the people in the industrial slums of London were as poor, hungry, and confined as his own people. There was no secret. When he returned home, the religion of his people had been outlawed. So Black Elk joined the Catholic Church. He prayed and read the Bible, and concluded that the Christian God and the Red God were One. And with equal commitment, he evangelized for Christ, and served as a Medicine Man. But nothing changed for his people.

50 continue

At 70, Black Elk was destitute, nearly blind, and worn out by grief and a sense of failure.

Now when I look about me upon my people in despair, I feel like crying and I wish and wish my Vision could have been given to a man more worthy.

I wonder why it came to me, a pitiful old man who can do nothing....the nation was dying, and the Vision was for the nation; but I have done nothing with it.

COMMENTARY

Black Elk's story was not yet finished. He lived to age 87. And his Vision was given new life.

On an August morning in 1930, John Neihardt, a Nebraska poet, drove up the dirt track to Black Elk's shack. Neihardt had heard about the old holy man and wanted to interview him. Black Elk stood in the open door. He'd felt this man's coming.

Black Elk invited Neihardt to stay, and put up a tipi next to his shack. Over four months, Black Elk told the story of his life, and Neihardt took notes. And for the first time, he told his great Vision. He had always held it close, guarding its power. But now, it would be put on paper and travel. It need not die with him.

Neihardt's book, Black Elk Speaks, was published in 1931. In it, Black Elk describes what he saw at the end of his Vision from Harney Peak. In the telling, it became clear to him that his dream was for all people:

> *I saw the sacred hoop of my people was one of many hoops that made one circle...*
>
> *and in the center grew one mighty flowering tree to shelter all the children of one mother and one father.*
>
> *If the vision was true and mighty, as I know, it is true and mighty yet.*

51

Gate A-4

by Naomi Shihab Nye

Wandering around the Albuquerque Airport Terminal, after learning my flight had been delayed four hours, I heard an announcement, "If anyone in the vicinity of Gate A-4 understands any Arabic, please come to the gate immediately."

Well – one pauses these days. Gate-4 was my own gate. I went there.

An older woman in full traditional Palestinian embroidered dress, just like my grandma wore, was crumpled to the floor, wailing. "Help" said the flight agent. "Talk to her. What is her problem? We told her the flight was going to be late and she did this."

I stooped to put my arm around the woman and spoke haltingly. "Shu-dow-a, shu-bid-uck, habibti? Stani schway, min fadlick, shu-bit-se-wee?" The minute she heard any words she knew, however poorly used, she stopped crying. She thought the flight had been cancelled entirely. She needed to be in El Paso for major medical treatment the next day. I said, "No, we're fine, you'll get there, just late, who is picking you up? Let's call him."

We called her son, I spoke with him in English. I told him I would stay with his mother till we got on the plane. She talked to him. Then we called her other sons just for the fun of it. Then we called my dad and he and she spoke for a while in Arabic and found out of course they had ten shared friends. Then I thought just for the heck of it why not call some Palestinian poets I know and let them chat with her? This all took up to two hours.

She was laughing a lot by then. Telling about her life, patting my knee, answering questions. She had pulled a sack of homemade mamool cookies – little powdered sugar crumbly mounds stuffed with dates and nuts – from her bag and was offering them to all the women

51 continue

at the gate. To my amazement, not a single traveler declined one. It was like a sacrament. The traveler from Argentina, the mom from California, the lovely woman from Laredo – we were all covered with the same powdered sugar. And smiling. There is no better cookie.

The airline broke out free apple juice and two little girls from our flight ran around serving it and they were covered with powdered sugar too. And I noticed my new best friend – by now we were holding hands – had a potted plant poking out of her bag, some medicinal thing, with green furry leaves. Such an old country traveling tradition. Always carry a plant. Always stay rooted to somewhere.

And I looked around that gate of late and weary ones and thought, this is the world I want to live in. The shared world. Not a single person in that gate – once the crying of confusion stopped – seemed apprehensive about any other person. They took the cookies. I wanted to hug all those other women too.

This can still happen anywhere. Not everything is lost.

COMMENTARY

Reading "Gate A-4," I recall how ridiculously high the ceilings are in airports, and how tiny and isolated I feel under all that air. And how, being watched, I turn into a watcher.

How could this possibly be the place that leads to what comes next?

Reading, I see the grandmother on the floor in her circle of skirts, and want to kneel and put back each thing that has spilled from her bag. I want to sit down inside her and see the Jerusalem she sees---its outside stairs and roof gardens, its desert air magnifying the traffic between worlds.

In this true story, an angel appears. She has a long braid and the eyes of a daughter. Her arm comforts, and the voices she calls up---sons, poets, friends of friends---make the grandmother's world familiar again.

Reading, I am given the secret: the real gate is not the fabled narrow one, but one wide enough for us all.

52

Billy Pilgrim is the main character in Kurt Vonnegut's novel *Slaughterhouse-Five*. He's 44, an optometrist, family man, and lives in a Midwestern town. He's also a WWII veteran who, as a German prisoner of war, was in Dresden the night of the Allied bombing.

In this scene, Billy is home alone sitting on the couch watching a late night movie on television. It's about American bombers in the Second World War. He becomes "slightly unstuck in time" and sees the movie *backwards*.

American planes, full of holes and wounded men and corpses took off backwards from an airfield in England. Over France, a few German fighter planes flew at them backwards, sucked bullets and shell fragments from some of the planes and crewmen. They did the same for wrecked American bombers on the ground, and those planes flew up backwards to join the formation.
The formation flew backwards over a German city that was in flames. The bombers opened their bomb bay doors, exerted a miraculous magnetism which shrunk the fires, gathered them into cylindrical steel containers, and lifted the containers into the bellies of the planes. The containers were stored neatly in racks. The Germans below had miraculous devices of their own, which were long steel tubes. They used them to suck more fragments from the crewmen and planes. But there were still a few wounded Americans, though, and some of the bombers were in bad repair. Over France, though, German fighters came up again, made everything and everybody as good as new.
When the bombers got back to their base, the steel cylinders were taken from the racks and shipped back to the United States of America, where factories were operating night and day, dismantling the cylinders, separating the dangerous contents into minerals. Touchingly, it was mainly women who did this work. The minerals were then shipped to specialists in remote areas. It was their business to put them into the ground, to hide them cleverly, so they would never hurt anybody ever again.

52 contiunue

The American fliers turned in their uniforms, became high school kids and Hitler turned into a baby, Billy Pilgrim supposed. That wasn't in the movie. Billy was extrapolating. Everybody turned into a baby, and all humanity, without exception, conspired biologically to produce two perfect people named Adam and Eve, he supposed.

COMMENTARY

It took Kurt Vonnegut 23 years before he was able to make a story of his experience of the fire-bombing of Dresden, February 13, 1945. On that night, he'd been locked-up with other American prisoners of war in an abandoned concrete slaughterhouse. In the morning, he emerged, a miraculous survivor, in an expanse of smoking ruins. A gray, soundless, lifeless afterworld. 135,000 people had been killed that night. Vonnegut's work was to push a wheelbarrow and pull out the dead---women, children, old men---and heave them onto a stack for burning.

∗∗∗

Watching the movie play backwards, Billy Pilgrim saw the harm his own kind had done, undone.

But Billy's fantasy didn't stop there. Continuing back, before the movie's first frame, he saw American fliers turn in their uniforms and become high school kids again, and all humanity become babies as far back as Adam and Eve.

Watching the movie play backwards, Billy Pilgrim arrived at the place where the first step is taken and from which all else follows. There, what is true in one heart is true of every heart. And there is only one rule: we must care for one another.

Sitting on the couch with Billy, "slightly unstuck in time," you and I can see what he saw: we can start again from scratch.

Bibliography/Credits

Epigram: William Stafford, excerpt from "A Ritual to Read to Each Other" from *Ask Me: 100 Essential Poems*. Copyright 1960, 2014 by William Stafford and the Estate of William Stafford. Reprinted with the permission of The Permissions Group, Inc. on behalf of Graywolf Press, Minneapolis, Minnesota, www.graywolfpress.org

1 *A Man Without A Country*, by Kurt Vonnegut, edited by Daniel Simon, Random House, New York, 2007, p 107

2 *Early Morning: Remembering My Father, William Stafford*, by Kim Stafford, Graywolf Press, Saint Paul, Minnesota, 2002, p 39

3 *The Brothers Karamazov*, by Fyodor Dostoevsky, translated by Richard Pevear and Larissa Volokhonsky, North Point Press, San Francisco, 1990, p 319. Commentary: ElderSpirit workshop, *practice for life*, Congregational UCC, Lincoln City, Oregon, by permission of John Schlorholtz

4 *The Road*, by Cormac McCarthy, Alfred A. Knopf, New York, 2006, pp 108,109,196 Commentary quotes from *Nuclear Tipping Point* (DVD), Nuclear Security Project, 2010

5 "The Giant and the Tailor," a folk tale, remembered and written by Charles Busch

6 South Texas Coffee Shop (personal anecdote), Commentary statistics from, *War No More* by David Swanson, Charlottesville, VA, 2013, pp 50, 141-2; William Stafford excerpts from *Every War Has Two Losers*, edited by Kim Stafford, (Milkweed Editions, 2003), pp 70, 27, 65. Copyright 2003 by Kim Stafford. Reprinted with the permission of The Permissions Group, Inc. on behalf of Kim Stafford, www.permissionsgroup.com

7 Cynical quotes: Joseph Stalin, Gen. Curtis LeMay, Latin proverb, Herman Goering, Major Booris, William Burroughs. Commentary quotes: Irving Greenberg, Yehuda Amichai

8 *My Dog Skip*, Warner Bros. Family Entertainment, 2000 Home Video, based on the novel by Willie Morris

9 *Jewish Encyclopedia*: Hillel the Elder (Shab. 31a) Commentary: *Daniel Berrigan, Essential Writings*, Orbis Books, Maryknoll, New York, 2009, pp 32, 33

10 *Ordinary Men, Reserve Police Battalion 101, The Final Solution in Poland*, by Christopher Browning, Harper Collins, New York, 1992 Commentary quote by David Ignatow by permission of Wesleyan University Press.

11 *Feather Fall, Laurens van der Post, An Anthology*, Edited by Jean-Marc Pottiez, William Morrow and Company, Inc., 1994, New York, p 55

12 *The New Oxford Annotated Bible*, RSV, Oxford University Press, 1952, New York, Genesis 4:1-16, pp 5-6

13 *The Road to Ramadii: The Private Rebellion of Staff Sargeant Camilo Mejia*, by Camilo Mejia, The New Press, 2007

14 *Passing Through: The Later Poems*, "Around Pastor Bonhoeffer," by Stanley Kunitz, W.W. Norton & Company, New York, 1995, pp 48,49 Commentary quotes from, Bonhoeffer, by Eric Metaxas, Thomas Nelson, Nashville, 2010

15 *A Man to Match His Mountains*, by Eknath Easwaran, Nilgiri Press, 1982, pp 110,111

16 Personal anecdote by Charles Busch

17 Adapted from *Thus Spoke Zarathustra*, by Friedrich Nietzsche, Barnes & Noble Classics, New York, 2005, pp 25, 26

18 Limited-Edition Broadside, Knight Library Press, Eugene, Oregon, 2004 *Pilgrim at Home, Vagabond Songs*, by Kim Stafford, "The Lucky Ones," Little Infinities, Portland, Oregon, 2009

19 *War Is A Racket*, by Major General Smedley Butler, Roundtable Press, 1935 Commentary quote: President Dwight D. Eisenhower's "Cross of Iron" speech to the American Society of Newspaper Editors, Washington, D.C., April 16, 1953

20 *Parabola, Storytelling and Education*, Vol IV, Number 4, November 1979, "Strung Memories," by Sister Maria Jose Hobday, p 6

21 *Gandhi: A Spiritual Biography*, by Arvind Sharma, Yale University Press, New Haven and London, 2013, p 151

22 *Two Wolves*, A Cherokee Legend, www.firstpeople.us

23 *Impact of Armed Conflict on Children, 5/28/2016*, by Graca Machel, UN Secretary Gerneral's Expert; *American Journal of Public Health, June 2014, 104(6):e34-337; Stanford Report*, January 24, 2011, Cynthia Haven quoting Richard Goldstone, former Justice of the Constitutional Court of South Africa.

24 *Jesus and Nonviolence, a Third Way*, by Walter Wink, Fortress Press, Minneapolis, 2003, pp 64, 65, 66

25 A personal anecdote by Charles Busch

26 *The Vocabulary of Peace*, by Shulamith Hareven, Mercury House, San Francisco, 1995, p 218

27 The Daily Show, hosted by Jon Stewart, October 10, 2013. Used with permission by Comedy Central 2018 Viacom Media Networks. All Rights Reserved. Comedy Central, all related titles, characters and logos are trademarks owned by Viacom Media Networks, a division of Viacom International Inc.

28 *Goodie Magazine* #38, 2008, Interview with Judith Malina, by Romy Ashby. Commentary: *Paradise Now*, 1968 production, New York City

29 *Peace Symposium*, Portland State University, Portland, Oregon, Prof. Cornel Pewewardy, 2013

30 Personal anecdote by Charles Busch. Commentary: *Conversations with Isaac Bashevis Singer*, by I.B. Singer and Richard Burgin, Farrar, Straus and Giroux, New York, pp 36, 53

31 "The Weight of the World," by Elizabeth Kolbert, The New Yorker, August 24, 2015 p 26. Commentary: *From War to Peace*, by Kent D. Shifferd, McFarland & Company, Inc., Publishers, Jefferson, North Carolina, 2011, p 147

32 An anecdote by Charles Busch based on a presentation by Don Eaton, Santa Fe, NM, by permission of Don Eaton

33 *The Autobiography of Philip Berrigan*, Common Courage Press, Monroe, ME, 1996, p 178

34 The Folk Tale, "Now I Am You," told by Charles Busch. Source unknown.

35 *Tao Te Ching*, #78, translated by Stephen Mitchell, Harper & Row, New York, 1988

36 A Vow of Nonviolence by Charles Busch

37 *Seeking Peace*, by Johann Christopher Arnold, "Foreward," by Madeleine L'Engle, Plough Publishing, Farmington, Pa, 2007, pp 6,7

38 *Peace Pilgrim, Her Life and Work in Her Own Words*, Compiled by some of her friends, An Ocean Tree Book, Santa Fe, New Mexico, 1983

39 Prophetic quotes from: William Stafford, Jody Williams, James Carroll, Dorothy Day, Abraham Joshua Heschel, Graca Machel, Martin Luther King, Jr.

40 *One Hundred Faces Of War Gives Soldiers A Voice*, NPR Weekend Edition, Sunday, May 30, 2010, Margo Adler. *Packing Inferno: The Unmaking of a Marine*, by Tyler E. Boudreau, Feral House, Port Townsend, WA, 2008, pp 189,190. Commentary: pp 170, 172, 158, 207,122

41 A Taoist folk tale told by Charles Busch. Commentary: *Ten Thousand Joys and Ten Thousand Sorrows*, Olivia Ames Hoblitzelle, Jeremy P. Tarcher/Penguin, New York, 2010, p 111

42 "Christmas Sermon on Peace," by Dr. Rev. Martin Luther King, Jr., December 24, 1967, At the Ebenezer Baptist Church, Atlanta, Georgia. Copyright 1967 by Dr. Martin Luther King. Jr., renewed 1995 Coretta Scott King. Commentary: *The New York Times Book Review*, Nov. 30, 1986, "Driven to Martydom," By Howell Raines, pp 3,33,34

43 2015 National Public Radio, Inc. Transcript of excerpt from NPR news report titled "Reckoning With Afghanastan's Toll" in *Green On Blue* as originally broadcast on NPR's *Weekend Edition Sunday* on February 22, 2015, and is used by the permission of NPR. Any unauthorized duplication is stricktly prohibited. Commentary: *Green on Blue*, by Elliot Ackerman, Scribner, New York, 2015, p 100

44 A personal anecdote, "Debts and Credits," by Charles Busch

45 *The Sabbath*, by Abraham Joshua Heschel, Farrar, Straus and Giroux, New York, 1951, pp 14,20,87

46 *No Strangers to Violence, No Strangers to Love*, by Boniface Hanley, O.F.M., Ave Maria Press, Notre Dame, Indiana, 1983, pp122, 129, 130, 137-8, 141, 144. Commentary: *Daniel Berrigan, Essential Writings*, Selected with an Introduction by John Dear, Orbis Books, Maryknoll, New York, 2009, p113, *Every War Has Two Losers, William Stafford on Peace and War,* Edited and with an Introduction by Kim Stafford, Milkweed Editions, Minneapolis, Minnesota, 2003, p131

47 A meditation by Charles Busch on Pope Francis' invitation to the Presidents of Israel and Palestine to pray with him in the Vatican Garden, June 8, 2014

48 *The Universal Declaration of Human Rights*, adapted by Charles Busch, from the "simplified form"

49 "Revenge," by Taha Muhammad Ali, from *Hymns and Quotes: New and Selected Poems and Translations*, Peter Cole (Farriar, Straus, and Giroux, 2017).

50 *Black Elk Speaks*, by John G. Neihard, 1961, University of Nebraska Press, Lincoln, pp2,43,184; *Black Elk*, by Joe Jackson, 2016, Farrar, Straus and Giroux, New York, pp 59,61

51 Naomi Shihab Nye, "Gate A-4" from Honeybee. Copyright 2008. By permission of the author 2013.

52 *Slaughterhouse-Five*, by Kurt Vonnegut, Dell Publishing, New York, 1969, pp 74,75

Praise for *soft as water*

soft as water is full of unusual wisdom, but with common threads across genres cultures, and centuries. You should be able to dip into it frequently for encouragement as well as strategic direction.

David Swanson
author of War Is A Lie, *and Director of* World Beyond War

This book is truly made of water—52 sips of wisdom, and with each, you will be lighter on your feet, more fluid in response to trouble, more likely to find humor, compassion, and curiosity when faced with the daily insults of these mysterious times. Peace can be concentric, and this book will start the ripples spreading outward from a new hunch for hope in you.

Kim Stafford
editor of Every War Has Two losers: William Stafford on Peace and War.

Each of the entertaining, challenging voices in *soft as water* remind us what our hearts know: only nonviolent solutions to conflict will bring peace. And today, peace is a matter of world survival.

David Hartsough
author, Waging Peace, *co-founder Nonviolent Peaceforce.*